FUNDY
NATIONAL PARK

A GUIDE TO
FUNDY
NATIONAL PARK

MICHAEL BURZYNSKI

Douglas & McIntyre
Vancouver/Toronto

Published in co-operation with Parks Canada
and the Canadian Government Publishing Centre,
Supply and Services Canada

Copyright © Minister of Supply and Services Canada 1985
Catalogue number R62-150/2-1984E

Douglas & McIntyre Ltd., 1615 Venables Street, Vancouver, British Columbia V5L 2H1

Canadian Cataloguing in Publication Data

Burzynski, Michael, 1954-
   Fundy National Park

      Bibliography: p.
      Includes index.
      ISBN 0-88894-458-6

      1. Fundy National Park (N.B.)–Guide-books.
2. Natural history–New Brunswick–Fundy
National Park.   I. Parks Canada.   II. Title.
FC2464.F95B87 1985   917.15'31   C85-091166-4
F1044.F92B87 1985

Maps by Evelyn Kirkaldy

Printed and bound in Canada by D. W. Friesen & Sons Ltd.

 Parks **Parcs**
       Canada **Canada**

CONTENTS

PREFACE
page 7

INTRODUCTION
page 8

BENEATH THE SCENERY
page 11

FOG ALONG THE FUNDY COAST
page 19

BAY OF THE GIANT TIDES
page 27

FOREST OF DARKNESS, FOREST OF LIGHT
page 39

RIVERSONG
page 63

WHEN THE TALL TREES FELL
page 75

FUNDY NATIONAL PARK
page 91

READING LIST
page 123

INDEX
page 125

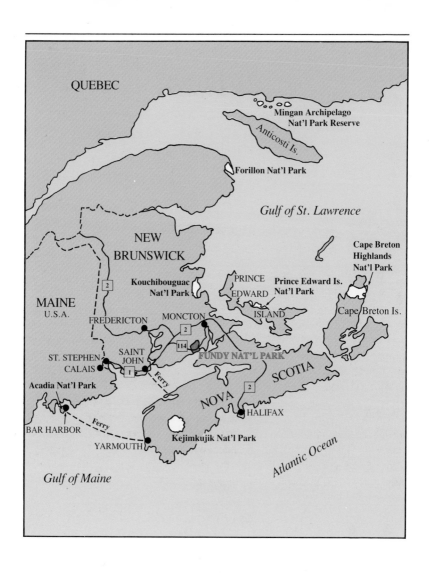

QUEBEC

Mingan Archipelago
Nat'l Park Reserve

Anticosti Is.

Forillon Nat'l Park

Gulf of St. Lawrence

NEW
BRUNSWICK

Cape Breton
Highlands
Nat'l Park

Kouchibouguac
Nat'l Park

PRINCE
EDWARD

Prince Edward Is.
Nat'l Park

MAINE
U.S.A.

ISLAND

Cape Breton Is.

2

FREDERICTON

MONCTON

2

114

SAINT
JOHN

FUNDY NAT'L PARK

ST. STEPHEN
CALAIS

1

SCOTIA

Ferry

Acadia Nat'l Park

NOVA

2

BAR HARBOR

Ferry

HALIFAX

YARMOUTH

Kejimkujik Nat'l Park

Atlantic Ocean

Gulf of Maine

PREFACE

Fundy — a short name for a small national park. A name that conjures up images of the bay of the giant tides, of dense spruce-fir forest, of rugged river valleys, and of a steep coastline washed by silty waves. Fundy is complex despite its size, and this guidebook has been written to try to answer some of the questions that you as a visitor or an armchair traveller might have about the park. The text outlines the major features and facilities of the park, and explains some of the most obvious phenomena. On another level, I hope that it will excite in you some of the feelings that I have for Fundy. After a dozen years of association with this park I am still discovering it. There are always new plants and animals to photograph, new waterfalls to swim beneath, new routes to explore — and everything changes with the seasons. I have always enjoyed seeing this park through the eyes of its visitors, and I can only hope that you enjoy seeing it through mine.

Michael Burzynski

INTRODUCTION

N o single place can capture the diversity of Canada with its mountains and prairies, tundra and forests, great rivers and lakes, stretching from the Atlantic to the Pacific and from the Great Lakes to the Arctic Ocean.

On the basis of climate, geology, and plant and animal communities, Canada can be divided into thirty-nine terrestrial and nine marine regions. By protecting a portion of each of these regions, examples of the most important landscapes that constitute the country's natural heritage will be safe forever. The process of protection began in 1885 when a tiny section of the Rocky Mountains was set aside by an Act of Parliament. Twenty-six square kilometres of mountain scenery and hot springs became Canada's first national park — Banff. Since then, a system of national parks has evolved, spanning the land from sea to sea to sea.

Each of Canada's national parks is a very special place. Locations are chosen only after years of study, with the final selection based on how well the site represents the surrounding area. So far, Canada has only thirty-one national parks. These represent twenty-eight of the forty-eight natural regions, but protect only 1.4 per cent of Canada's land area.

Once land is granted national park status, it becomes an island in a sea of change. We may farm, lumber, mine and build all around it, but the park must remain natural. Canadian law decrees that the mandate of Parks Canada is ''to protect for all time those places which are significant examples of Canada's natural and cultural heritage, and to encourage public understanding, appreciation and enjoyment of this heritage in ways which leave it unimpaired for future generations.''

Parks Canada preserves representative portions of our wild landscape and also manages heritage canals, and national historic parks and sites.

Fundy National Park was established in 1948. Although small when compared to many of Canada's other national parks, it is remarkably diverse. Thirteen kilometres of park cliffs and beaches skirt the Bay of Fundy, the bay with the world's greatest tides. Inland, the park protects a portion of deeply valleyed plateau blanketed with a forest of spruce, fir, birch and maple — the Acadian Forest of the Caledonia Highlands. Fundy's 206 km² comprise some of the most beautiful country in southern New Brunswick, and are a preserved example of the Maritime Acadian Highlands, an extension of the ancient Appalachian Mountains.

This guidebook is being launched as Canada celebrates the hundredth anniversary of its national parks. The first section of the book presents the natural and human stories of the park; the second section describes facilities, programs and trails, and offers the visitor suggestions and advice. It has been designed as an introduction to one particular park, an exploration of its features and its surroundings, and as a souvenir of a visit.

Canada is a vast country. The best way to explore it is through its national park system.

BENEATH THE SCENERY

T he rocks that underlie Fundy have travelled farther to get where they are than most of the park's visitors, and their journey has been a traveller's nightmare. Wandering aimlessly for eons, the rocks have experienced head-on collisions, have sunk beneath the sea then resurfaced, and have overheated and frozen. They bear all the signs of the wrenches, wrinkles and scrapes that they have received, and are, for the time being, parked and recovering in southern New Brunswick. How all of this happened, and how the park's rocks evolved, is a long story — about 700 million years long.

CONTINENTS IN COLLISION

The cool, hard surface of the earth on which we live is only a thin crust afloat on a sphere of partly molten rock. Movements within the earth's semi-liquid interior create huge cracks in its crust and cause continent-sized plates of rock to drift apart and collide with each other. As they ever so slowly collide, wrinkles the size of mountain chains are forced up along their edges. The plates ride over and under each other, break up and reassemble, rearranging themselves into the features that we know as the face of the earth. This process began about four billion years ago when the molten earth had lost enough heat for a crust of rock to harden on its surface. The cracking and shifting continues to this day, moving continents and raising mountains, all accompanied by earthquakes and volcanic eruptions where the movements are greatest.

We do not live long enough as individuals or even as cultures to observe the inexorable migrations and collisions of continents, but we can read their story in the rocks. Unfortunately, the older rocks are, the more contorted and changed they are, and this makes exploring their history more difficult and less precise.

The most ancient rocks in Fundy are about 750 million years old, dating back to a time (the Precambrian) when the seas held all of the earth's primitive life. What is now southern New Brunswick was then part of an arc of volcanic islands in the middle of an ocean, much like the modern-day Japanese archipelago.

Across a shallow sea to the northwest, the Canadian Shield was forming, and southeast across a deep ocean trench was land that is now Morocco and Europe.

For millions of years, sediments washed from the lifeless, eroding islands and accumulated in thick beds offshore. These ancient, hard red sandstones and conglomerates are now visible in the banks of the middle Point Wolfe River. Volcanic eruptions poured lava and ash into the sea and over the sediments. These became the andesites and tuffs visible on the west side of Point Wolfe cove. Movements of the earth's interior forced the crust apart, opening a major rift to the north of the islands. These islands remained attached to the rock plate that would one day become Morocco and Europe. The North American plate slowly, slowly drifted away, and an ocean opened.

Over the following 100 million years (Cambrian-Ordovician), this ocean — the Iapetus — widened, and the volcanic islands were pushed eastward, eventually colliding with the Morocco and European plate. The pressure and heat of this slow collision buckled the ocean sediments as if they were modelling clay. Magma (molten rock) was squeezed into the folds and cracks that developed in the rock-hard sediments, and, on cooling, it crystallized (hardened) to form granites and diorites, some of which are now exposed in the park at Big Dam on the Broad River and beneath the covered bridge on the Fortyfive River.

The next great period of change, from 435 to 395 million years ago (Silurian), saw the geological conveyor belt change direction, and the North American and European plates start to creep towards each other. By 395 million years ago (Devonian), the Iapetus Ocean had completely closed, and the rocks that would become southern New Brunswick were once again attached to the rest of North America.

The collision that accompanied the closing of the Iapetus Ocean caused extensive folding, faulting, melting and compression of the rocks, and major mountain ranges were thrust up. This episode of mountain building, the Acadian Orogeny, formed the Appalachian Mountain range along the northeast edge of North America as well as a system of mountains in Eastern Europe, Greenland and Scandinavia. There were few land plants at this time to hold the soil, so erosion was rapid. As the mountains wore down, their sediments were swept by rivers into the valleys where they accumulated in thick layers on top of the older rocks. Examples of these Devonian sediments outcrop near St. Andrews, New Brunswick, and in the Cobequid Mountains of Nova Scotia.

Neuropteris, *an ancient fern preserved in Boss Point sandstone*

Following a period of mountain building, there is often a relaxing of pressure during which parts of mountain chains sink along large cracks (faults) in the earth's crust and form rift valleys (Figure 1). About 350 million years ago, the Bay of Fundy was born of this phenomenon. As the land slowly sank, fans of sediments washed into the rift valley. Other sediments settled in a large marshy lake in what is now the Hillsborough area. These muds, rich in plant and animal matter, eventually became the Albert oil shales, which contain oil and natural gas and small fish fossils.

The rift valley was briefly flooded by a warm shallow sea (Figure 2). Sediments deposited during this period are now limestones containing fossils of coral reefs and coral-like algae, denizens of tropical seas. Parts of this sea became cut off from open water and eventually dried out under the hot sun. Mineral salts left behind by the evaporating sea water became the rock salt at Windsor, N.S., the gypsum at Hillsborough, N.B., and the potash at Sussex, N.B. Eventually, the sea retreated, and intermittent rains washed debris down from the surrounding highlands, covering the marine deposits with a cap of rock (Figure 3). The coarse iron-rich sediments turned rusty-brown in the hot dry air. Over millions of years, the mountains eroded and the valleys filled layer by layer. The iron acted as a glue, welding sand, gravel and rocks tightly together to form today's Hopewell Conglomerate, as seen at Herring Cove, Point Wolfe and Hopewell Cape (The Rocks).

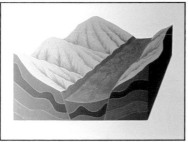

Fig. 1: Rift valley

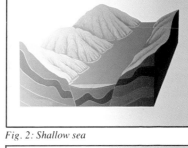

Fig. 2: Shallow sea

Fig. 3: Desert-like conditions

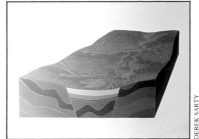

Fig. 4: Coal-age swamps

DEREK SARTY

Over the next fifteen million years, drifting of the continental plates carried the southern New Brunswick rocks to the equator, and erosion reduced the uplands to low, rolling hills (Figure 4). Valleys filled with the fine sands and mud carried by wide, meandering rivers. Lush forests of giant ferns, horsetails and primitive conifers blanketed the marshy lowlands, thriving in the humidity and heat. Insects flew among the trees while large amphibians, ancient relatives of frogs and salamanders, prowled the swamps in search of food. Southern New Brunswick was then a lush tropical swamp, but all that remains today are fossils. Carbonized by heat and time, and pressed into thin bands and coal seams, the plant fossils of this period give it its name: the Coal Age (Carboniferous). Within the park — where of course collecting is prohibited — fossils may be seen at Herring Cove and Cannontown (swimming pool) beach. Joel Head, Owls Head and Cape Enrage near Alma bear thin coal seams. The most impressive local fossil site is at Joggins, N.S., just across the Bay of Fundy, where there are fossil trees the size of today's spruces. These blue-grey to buff fossil-bearing sandstones and shales predate dinosaurs by almost 100 million years.

About 250 million years ago, the giant plate of rock that would eventually become Africa bumped into the North American and European plates, and another period of mountain-building began. As a tablecloth is wrinkled by a push from the side, so the Alleghenian Orogeny forced the rocks along the edge of the plates into a complex series of folds, shattering some

Fig. 5: Volcanoes erupt

Fig. 6: Land tilts; drainage changes

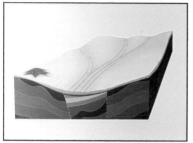

Fig. 7: Last ice-age scours the land

Fig. 8: Present Bay of Fundy

into faults and thrusts. The rusty Hopewell Conglomerate at Point Wolfe and Herring Cove and the Boss Point sandstones at Cape Enrage which were originally deposited on the horizontal now tilt almost straight up and down because of this collision.

By 225 million years ago (Triassic), all of the drifting continental plates had ground up against one another and combined into a "super continent" known to geologists as Pangaea. The sediments that filled the Bay of Fundy rift valley during this period became the brick-red sandstones and shales of Waterside, Martin Head and St. Martins, N.B.

The Atlantic Ocean was born about 165 million years ago (late Triassic, early Jurassic), when a new rift opened in the earth's crust. Widening by several centimetres each year (as it does to this day), it filled with sea water. Tension in the earth's crust caused by these movements led to the eruption of a chain of low volcanoes along the northwest coast of Nova Scotia, in the Digby area. Over millenia, numerous eruptions spewed layer after layer of fluid basalt lava over the Bay of Fundy rift (Figure 5). These basalts can be seen today at Ile Haute, Brier Island, Cape Split and Cap d'Or in Nova Scotia, and on Grand Manan Island in New Brunswick.

Widening of the Atlantic continued, but volcanic activity ceased (Jurassic-Cretaceous) as the European and North American continents drifted farther apart. Movements of the earth's crust tilted what is now the upper bay and reversed the direction of drainage in the Bay of Fundy rift. Rivers carved out new valleys that foretold the shape of today's bay (Figure 6).

Sculpted rocks and waterfalls line the Broad River

DEEP FREEZE

About one-and-a-half million years ago the climate of the earth cooled as it had done again and again in the past. More snow fell during the winters than melted during the short, cool summers. Snow accumulated, its own bulk squeezing its lower layers into ice. For a million years the land was engulfed by a series of ice ages (Figure 7).

Continental glaciers several kilometres thick flowed under their own weight as gravity pulled them towards sea level. Chunks of rock, frozen into the undersides of the ice sheets, raked across the land. Gouging and tearing at the old landscape, they gradually sculpted a new one.

About 13 500 years ago, a warming trend ended the last ice age. As more snow melted than fell during the course of a year, the ice sheets began to shrink. Billions of tonnes of meltwater flowed over the landscape, wearing tunnels and valleys in the ice and loosening sand, gravel and boulders. Water, as if excited to be free again, roared in muddy, frothing torrents over, through and under the deteriorating ice, across the lowlands and to the sea. Wherever the rivers slackened on their charge to the sea, their tumbling loads of debris were dropped. River valleys filled with gravel and boulders, and outwash fans built up where the torrents dumped sand and mud into the bay.

BOUNCING BACK

The immense weight of the ice sheet had depressed the land, forcing it below sea level. As its burden melted away with the end of the ice age, the land slowly rose again (Figure 8). River-mouth fans were lifted out of the water and the rivers cut channels down through them. The gravel terraces on which the village of Alma and the park's Headquarters Campground are built were both part of ancient underwater outwash fans, but are now tens of metres above sea level. Glacial features throughout the Headquarters Area have been modified by landscaping, but often this serves to outline rather than to obscure them. Stripped of trees and reclothed in closely cropped lawn, the grassy bowl and MacLaren Pond betray their origin as a glacial kettle. Smaller dry kettleholes, left by chunks of the melting ice sheet, lie hidden in the nearby woods. Kame terraces — layer upon layer of water-borne rock debris deposited alongside a stagnant arm of a glacier — form the tiers on which the golf course is built. Everywhere, glacial till lies just beneath the surface of the soil.

Geological processes did not end with the ice age. Erosion has changed much since then, along the shore, up the rivers, and over the entire surface of the land. Even now the Upper Salmon River is adding to its present delta fan, spreading it farther out into the bay. The surface of the flats marks sea level today as the terraces that look down on it did in the past. Another potent geological force is people. Landscaping, gravel extraction, lake and river damming, mining, road building, and altering of drainage patterns — all have occurred within the park area and have left their mark. Geological time marches on, and we are part of it.

FOG ALONG THE FUNDY COAST

P rovincial weather reports give the Fundy coast a bad reputation. At the end of each cheery summer prediction of warmth and sun comes the caution ". . . but foggy along the Fundy coast," or ". . . five degrees cooler along the Fundy coast." But reality is not nearly so gloomy. The sunburn fraternity can have the steamier portions of the province; those of us who prefer variable weather, moderate temperatures and summer nights cool enough for sleep prefer the Fundy shore.

A CLIMATE FROM THE BAY

The Bay of Fundy is responsible for most local weather conditions and for the moderate bay-shore climate as a whole. Surface water of the upper bay has an average summer temperature of 14°C, a few degrees warmer than at the mouth. Winter temperatures are reversed, with oceanic water warming the mouth of the bay to slightly above the 2°C experienced at its head. The large body of water is therefore much cooler than the surrounding land during the summer and often warmer during the winter. Air passing over the bay is either warmed or cooled by it, which accounts for many weather variations and such phenomena as cool breezes, fog and sea smoke.

As the land warms up during a summer's day, the air above it also warms and rises. Cooler, denser air from the bay floods in across beaches, fields and forests to replace it. The land warms the new air and the process continues, creating sea breezes. The cooling effect of these sea breezes is greatest during the afternoon and early evening. As the sun sets and the earth passes into darkness, the land cools faster than the bay, and the process is reversed; cool land air flows out over the bay creating land breezes.

Air warmed by the land during the day picks up moisture. As it drifts out over the bay, the air is cooled and sinks closer to the water surface. Moisture is forced out of the cooling air in the form of droplets light enough to be buoyed up by the air. The mist of droplets floats and swirls and drifts as it grows, eventually forming a bank of fog over the surface of the bay. Pushed by a light wind or displaced by more cooling and sinking air, the fog is forced up over the land where it will stay until dissipated by sun and wind. Fog often forms with the rising tide and will settle over the coastline in late evening or early morning and last until well after noon. Driving down into it sometimes gives one the impression of plunging into a wall of cotton batting. It is not unusual for visitors in the park's coastal campgrounds to be groping around in a swirling mist while those on the plateau are basking in sunshine.

Sheltered as it is between New Brunswick and Nova Scotia, the upper bay rarely builds up waves of any consequence. Often the water is dead calm, rising and falling with the tides but showing no hint of waves or swell. On still days, mirages sometimes form. The cliffs of Nova Scotia mirrored by the water will seem twice as high. A layer of cold air will pool just above the water, with reflections shimmering and sliding about its surface. Faraway objects may be distorted beyond recognition; islands and boats seem to hover high above the water.

A MATTER OF DEGREES

Two distinct climatic zones exist within the park. The climate of the coastal area, moderated by the bay, consists of cool summers, mild winters, and frequent fog during the warmer months. On the upland plateau the summers are warmer and the winters colder. Not only does more snow fall inland, but it lasts longer there too. Fog, however, is much less frequent. During the summer, sea breezes can lower the temperature along the coast by as much as 6°C compared to inland. Other differences are shown in the following table:

	Park Coast (Headquarters)	Park Interior (Wolfe Lake)
Mean Annual Number of Frost-Free Days	147	102
Mean Annual Temperature	5.3°C	3.8°C
Mean Annual Rainfall	1186 mm	1211 mm
Mean Annual Snowfall*	224 mm	384 mm
Extreme Temperatures — Maximum	30°C (July)	37.5°C (May)
Average Summer Temperature (July and August)	21°C	22°C
Extreme Temperatures — Minimum	–30°C (Feb.)	–36°C (Jan.)
Average Winter Temperature (January and February)	–1.4°C	–4.5°C

* Snowfall is expressed in mm of water; the actual depth of the snow would be ten times greater (i.e. 224 cm and 384 cm)

The mean annual temperature (the average of all daily temperatures for a year) for the park is very similar to that of Ottawa (5.8°C) and Quebec City (5.3°C) but somewhat lower than that of Vancouver (10.1°C). It is also interesting to compare mean annual rainfall and snowfall in the park to other parts of Canada: Halifax receives 1108 mm of rain and 211 mm of snow; Vancouver receives 1181 mm of rain and 49 mm of snow, and Ottawa, a paltry 649 mm of rain and 141 mm of snow.

Total precipitation for the park averages about 1408 mm, with 55 to 60 per cent of the days of the year overcast and cloudy. This is not as dismal as it sounds, since fully one-half of the days of summer will be sunny. (Indeed in some recent summers the park has gone without rain or fog for up to a month.) The only hitch is that for almost half of the days in July (less in other months) it is foggy along the coast.

The greatest snowfall recorded over a twenty-four-hour period was 47 cm; such snowfalls contribute to the popularity of the park with cross-country skiers and snowshoers. One thing that winter visitors must keep in mind, however, is that even though the coastal part of the park is warmer than inland, biting winds off the bay lower the temperature and can chill anyone outside the protection of the forest. Winds throughout the year have a westerly component, and storms are possible at any time but are most frequent during the winter when they are also more severe. Occasionally during the autumn the park area is affected by the edges of hurricanes, tropical storms from the Caribbean that cause very heavy rainfall.

THE GROUNDHOG DAY GALE

Although the surface of the bay can be mirror-smooth for days at a time, wind can quickly pile up waves. Twisted trees along the cliff tops and others inland toppled in rows by the fury of gales testify to the power of air. Water has 800 times more mass than air, and consequently, moving water can do even more damage. On 2 February 1976, a storm that has come to be known as the Groundhog Day Gale ripped through southern New Brunswick and Nova Scotia. The normally placid upper bay became a roiling, seething maelstrom. The storm worsened as the ride rose, sending waves crashing onto the road between the park and Alma and onto the swimming pool parking lot. No boats were in the water because of the time of year, so they were spared, but the Alma wharf and breakwater were pounded to pieces. Had the tide been higher and had the wind driven the waves directly on shore, severe damage would have been done to the town, but the tide turned and the storm slackened as it moved on, leaving considerable wreckage in its wake. Trees more than a mile inland were damaged by salt spray, and sections of budworm-weakened forest were flattened. Beach rocks of more than one hundred kilograms were found lying in the middle of the road, and pieces of wharf littered the beach. A small freshwater marsh on Alma Beach was breached by the sea, and all of its plants and animals were swept out to sea, as was a boardwalk that spanned the marsh. The wave-scoured bases of gravel cliffs became unstable and began to slump. To protect park buildings and a road in the Headquarters Area, large boulders were subsequently placed along the cliff bases to slow their collapse and to buffer them against further gales.

The Groundhog Day Gale certainly left its mark, as did its predecessor, the Saxby Gale of 1869, and as will storms yet to come. Weather of this sort is particularly memorable in the upper bay because it occurs so rarely. When you look across at Nova Scotia's cliffs mirrored in the bay, remember that there are waves in that calm sea just waiting to be released — waves and currents that will continue to mould the shoreline, no matter how hard we try to resist them.

THROUGH THE SEASONS

Since constantly mixing bay water rarely cools to the $-2°C$ necessary for it to freeze, the bay usually remains ice-free throughout the winter. Sometimes parts of the extreme upper bay ice over, but tides quickly break the ice into large cakes that shift en masse with the wind. Sometimes they pile up on the park shore, beaching on the mudflats at low tide like so many icebergs. High tide refloats them and they plough across the gravel and mud as they move. Next day, if the wind changes, they may be seen only as a faint white band plastered against the base of the cliffs on the Nova Scotia shore.

Chill winter air can cool beach boulders to well below zero degrees. As the tide rises, water freezes around the rocks forming a thin, patterned crust of opaque ice. Layer by layer, the ice builds with each tide until the whole upper beach is glazed with a hard white mantle.

Sea smoke is a winter phenomenon. On days when the air temperature falls well below that of bay water, water vapour will rise and saturate the air above the bay. Cooled, the vapour condenses, and wisps and curls of mist, spaced like ghostly pillars, hover low over the water surface as far as the eye can see.

In winter, fogs and mists sometimes settle over the forest at night. By morning large feathery crystals of hoar frost have turned the trees into a sparkling dream-forest, but they are soon blown asunder by the day's first gusts of wind.

Storms of freezing rain create a different effect. Cold drizzle freezes around branches and trunks. Trees bow low under the weight of accumulating ice, and soon the forest looks as though it is made of spun glass. The silence is broken only by the cracking of strained branches and the tinkle of shattering ice. Sunlight dances across these crystal forests and is

Fog rising over Joel Head

splintered into rainbows of colour by ice prisms. An ice storm leaves behind an awesome beauty, but is a tremendous hazard to the trees and animals that must endure it.

Weather can have a strong effect on the plants and animals of the park in a general way too: animals sometimes freeze during winter rains, and trees may collapse under the burden of ice and snow. A long, hard winter of cold weather and deep snow will force deer, and sometimes even moose, to collect in yards — sheltered areas where food is abundant and the trampling of moving animals packs the snow into hard paths. As the winter wears on and food becomes scarce, animals may starve in large numbers, unable to muster the energy to plough through unpacked snow to new feeding grounds. Deep snow, brittle crusts and slick ice also make escape difficult for deer pursued by predators. Warm dry springs enhance the survival of insects such as spruce budworm caterpillars, hence the amount of summer defoliation is likely to be greater. Cool moist springs encourage the fungi that parasitize caterpillars.

Mouth of Upper Salmon River

Despite the coldness of bay waters, warm summer days always encourage people to paddle and swim. Bay water can best be described as invigorating. If one swims during the rising ride at Alma Beach, or outside the park at Dennis or Waterside beaches, the water will have absorbed heat from the sun-baked sand and gravel flats, and can be surprisingly pleasant.

During the summer, cool, moist coastal air keeps the forest green and fire-free even in periods of drought. Moisture-loving lichens, mosses and ferns drape from every available cliff face and tree trunk, and the decay of fallen trees is relatively rapid. On the evidence of charcoal layers deposited in bogs over the last few thousand years, the Bay of Fundy coastal forest has always had the lowest fire frequency in the province.

Autumn lingers. Cool nights and shortening days start the chemistry that changes tree leaves from the verdure of summer to the palette of fall. Birds flock, feeding and roosting by day or leap-frogging restlessly from tree to tree down the coast. By night they fly, a murmur of chirps punctuating the dark sky as unseen flocks pass overhead. Biting flies disappear, and tree leaves begin to thin out with the progress of Indian Summer. One's senses seem amplified, as if it is important to sample everything before the stillness of winter sets in. On woodland trails the air is heavy with the smell of leaves that crackle underfoot. Sweet scents of fern fronds, of loam and of crumbling stumps drift on every breeze. Without the buffer of foliage, winds seem windier and the sun cooler but sunnier. In the rivers, the salmon begin their preparations for spawning. Light frosts fringe the leaves that still cling to trees and bushes, a gentle reminder of winter's imminence.

Yes, it is a bit cooler along the Fundy coast, but that can be a blessing. Fog does sometimes obscure the view, but it can be beautiful while it lasts. Two important pieces of advice that apply here are: "If you don't like the weather, just wait awhile," and "There's no bad weather, just bad clothing." Remember, in Fundy the grass is *always* greener.

Acid Rain

It is an unfortunate quirk of fate that large air masses tend to sweep across central and eastern North America in such a direction that they funnel directly over the Northeastern States and the Atlantic Provinces before moving out to sea. On their journey they pick up gasses and particulate matter from the most heavily industrialized cities on the continent. Carried in the atmosphere for thousands of miles, these wastes are changed by sunlight and contact with other elements in the air to form acids. Sulphuric and nitric acid fall in rain and snow, and build up the acidity of soil and water bodies. Acid precipitation has exacted a ghastly toll of dead lakes and rivers, declining forests and wildlife. As yet, the soils and waters of Fundy National Park seem to have buffered this deadly airborne attack, but rivers and lakes in southwestern New Brunswick and nearby Nova Scotia already show signs of failure. Frogs, toads and salamanders are particularly sensitive to high acid levels in their breeding ponds, and for this reason are a good indicator of acid damage to a lake, pond or river. These amphibians are being monitored closely for adverse reactions, though not much can be done once acids build up. The only long-term solution is to reduce the problem at its source — the exhaust of automobiles and the air-borne wastes of industrial plants and power-generating stations.

BAY OF THE GIANT TIDES

W hether its name came from the Portuguese word for "deep" (fundo), or from the Portuguese or French for "split" (fenda, fendu) the Bay of Fundy is both. Plunging to 212 m (116 fathoms) at its mouth, it shallows to only 55 m (30 fathoms) off the coast of the park. At its head, the bay splits into two narrow arms — Chignecto Bay and Minas Basin.

It is neither the largest nor the deepest bay in the world, but the Bay of Fundy does have the world's greatest tidal variation. The twice daily rise and fall of its waters is like a heartbeat, giving the bay a life and character different from all other bodies of water. Everything associated with the bay, from coastline to climate and from seaweeds to fishermen, is profoundly affected by its tides.

From its mouth to its deeply forked head, the bay is about 290 km long. The shoreline of the lower bay is for the most part composed of low rocky headlands, boulder beaches, coves and islands. Towards the head of the bay this changes as towering cliffs, mud flats and salt marshes become more evident.

Before settlement, one of the world's largest acreages of salt marsh drained into the Bay of Fundy, kept fertile and lush by the giant tides. Millions of ducks, geese and other birds fed and nested in these marshes or used them as migration stops. Fish foraged and grew in the briny creeks, and uncountable smaller organisms flourished in the rich mud and marsh waters where nutrients from the land and sea came together to produce excellent growing conditions. Water flowing out of the marshes carried plant and animal matter, both dead and live — a source of food for animals in the upper bay.

In 1605 came the first attempt at permanent European settlement of the bay. Shortly thereafter farmers began to erect protective dykes to keep salt water off the marshes. Now, where waterfowl once dabbled, most of the salt marshes have been turned into pastures and cattle graze.

Within the park, the small salt marsh at the mouth of the Upper Salmon River and those on the Point Wolfe and Goose rivers were never farmed or dyked. When compared to the expanses of tidal meadow farther up the bay they seem insignificant, but they serve as reminders of the land that greeted the first settlers almost 400 years ago.

THE CADENCE OF THE TIDES

Perhaps the most vivid demonstration of the difference between the upper Bay of Fundy and other seacoasts can be found in the simple act of walking to the water's edge. If your timing is correct, it is possible to leave your car near Alma Beach, walk three or four steps from the roadside, and be ankle-deep in sea water. If your timing is off by six hours and a bit, you will have to walk more than a kilometre over boulders, gravel flats, sandbars and mud to wet your feet in the same water. Once there, you will be standing as much as 13 m below the sea level of six hours ago; in effect, you are walking on the bottom of the sea.

"What causes the tides?" is probably the most frequently asked question in the park. A simple answer is that the tides are caused by the gravitational pull of the sun and moon acting on water on the surface of the earth. Large bodies of water are set in regular, wavelike motion, and rise and fall twice daily along coastlines. The rise and fall of the North Atlantic is channelled into the Bay of Fundy where the size and shape of the bay amplify it and create giant tides at the head of the bay.

A more complete answer follows:

As the earth and moon move through space, they revolve slowly around a common centre of gravity, like uneven weights on a dumbbell. The gravity of these two planets and a force due to their rotation combine to create tide-generating forces that affect water on the surface of the earth. These forces are strongest at the point on the earth that is closest to the moon (Z), and at the point farthest away (N) (Figure 9).

As the earth turns during a day, different places on its surface pass into and out of points Z and N. Since the moon orbits slowly in the same direction as the earth spins, it takes slightly longer than an earth day for a place to reappear at point Z or N. This period of twenty-four hours and fifty minutes is the lunar or tidal day.

The tide-generating forces are weak, causing only a slight movement of water towards whichever point, Z or N, is closest at the time. During a tidal day, water molecules in any one place move about 170 m towards the west, then the east, then the west, and again to the east (Figure 9). The net effect of this east-west rocking, or looping, is a sloshing of water masses within basins. Also, due to the earth's rotation, there is an "apparent force" at work — the Coriolis Effect — by which a moving object in the

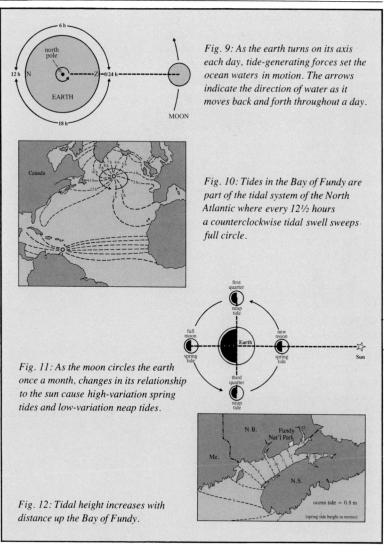

Fig. 9: As the earth turns on its axis each day, tide-generating forces set the ocean waters in motion. The arrows indicate the direction of water as it moves back and forth throughout a day.

Fig. 10: Tides in the Bay of Fundy are part of the tidal system of the North Atlantic where every 12½ hours a counterclockwise tidal swell sweeps full circle.

Fig. 11: As the moon circles the earth once a month, changes in its relationship to the sun cause high-variation spring tides and low-variation neap tides.

Fig. 12: Tidal height increases with distance up the Bay of Fundy.

Northern Hemisphere tends to the right, and in the Southern Hemisphere, to the left. Combined with the sloshing of water in ocean basins, this effect results in an apparent slow rotation of the water masses. In the North Atlantic this gyration is counterclockwise, and two complete sweeps of the basin are made each tidal day (Figure 10). There is no actual circulation of water around the ocean. The situation is similar to that of a tray of jello that is given a quick twist. A wave-like crest moves around the tray, but no jello molecules are permanently displaced; each merely oscillates around a point.

As the small crest of the ocean tide sweeps around the coast of the North Atlantic twice each tidal day, a place on the coast, such as Alma Beach, will have a change of tides about every six and a quarter hours. Thus there are two high and two low tides each tidal day.

The sun is much larger than the moon, but also much farther from the earth. On the west side of the Atlantic, its influence on the tides is one-fifth that of the moon. Twice each month the gravitational pulls of the sun and moon are in line — at the new moon and at the full moon (Figure 11). This causes spring tides: tide cycles with a larger than normal variation in height between high and low tide. (The name is derived from the Old English word ''springan'' meaning ''a welling.'') Also twice each month, at the quarter moons, the gravitational pull of the moon is at a right angle to that of the sun. This causes neap tides: tide cycles with a relatively small variation in height between high and low tide. (The name comes from another Old English word ''nep'' meaning ''scant'' or ''lacking,'' akin to ''nipped in the bud.'')

When the tide comes in on Alma Beach, it rises fast enough to catch up with a slow walker. If you stand at the water's edge for three minutes, your feet will be covered. If you remain there, in an hour the water will have crept up and over your body until only bubbles mark your place.

Few have the endurance to try this experiment. Most just wet their feet, then retreat leisurely up the beach. The water slowly follows, flooding the low areas and gurgling into clam and worm holes, rising until the vast mud and gravel flats are once more under the sea.

Tides in the Bay of Fundy are part of the tidal system of the North Atlantic. As the ocean level rises with the tide, water floods into the bay. As the ocean tide falls, water rushes out. In this way about 100 km³ of water surges into and out of the bay with each change of tides, a volume equal to the daily discharge of all of the rivers in the world.

The mouth of the bay is wide open to the Atlantic, and the rise and fall of ocean tides pumps energy into its waters. The result is a slow, steady rocking motion or seiche. The dimensions of the bay cause the seiche to coincide with, and reinforce, the tidal flow of ocean water as it enters and leaves the bay. In almost the same way that a gentle push at the right moment will keep a child on a swing moving, the ocean tide gives a push each day to the seiche in the bay. The coincidence of these two water movements causes the giant tides.

The Bay of Fundy and the Gulf of Maine are linked as a tidal system. The tides start to gain height at the edge of the continental shelf and increase up the length of the bay (Figure 12). In this way, during a spring tide, the 0.8-m tide of the open ocean is increased to as much as 16 m in Minas Basin and 15.2 m in Chignecto Bay. Along the coast of Fundy National Park the average tidal range is 9 m, with a neap tide range of 6 m

Left: high tide at Herring Cove; right: low tide at Herring Cove 6½ hours later

and a spring tide range of over 13 m. Some other places in the world with tidal ranges of about 10 m are: the Port of Bristol in southwest England; the Sea of Okhotsk, northeast of Japan; Turnagain Arm, near Anchorage, Alaska; the Bay of St. Malo, in Brittany, and the Leaf River in Ungava Bay, Quebec.

The tides of the Bay of Fundy developed as the glaciers of the last ice age melted. It is thought that about 6000 years ago a relative rise in sea level flooded the banks at the mouth of the bay and connected the bay to the Atlantic, bringing tides to the bay. Since then, tides have been increasing in range by 15 cm each century. In time, as sea level fluctuates and natural and man-induced changes alter the dimensions of the Bay of Fundy–Gulf of Maine system, its seiche will go out of phase with the ocean tides. Then the giant tides will be no more.

SHORELINE IN RETREAT

Muddy water is as characteristic of the upper Bay of Fundy as are the tides, and they are in some ways related. For millennia the reddish sandstone and conglomerate cliffs that contain the upper bay have been eroded by water. Chunks fall to the beaches below, there to be pounded and rolled by waves and abraded against other rocks. Small particles break off — sand and mud grains free again after hundreds of million of years — stained rusty brown by the iron that bound them in place. As the tide rises and falls, it stirs up mud that has settled on the beaches, and the mud swirls and mixes with the near-shore water. All along the shoreline a band of muddy water churns with each change of tide.

Mud has accumulated in deposits tens of metres thick in some parts of the upper bay. Held in place by salt marsh plants, the glutinous expanses are carved by a twisting network of creeks. Clouds of mud are discharged from the mouths of large tidal rivers such as the Petitcodiac and Memramcook. Close to shore, the mud never completely settles, no matter how calm the bay. For this reason, little light reaches the bottom of the upper bay, even in the shallows. In fact, 99 per cent of the sunlight at the water's surface is filtered out at a depth of only one metre.

Although the tides bring waves high up on the beaches, they also protect the shore. The Bay of Fundy is sheltered between Nova Scotia and New Brunswick, and the only lengthy reach is from the southwest. Storm winds rarely blow from that direction, so large waves and rough seas are uncommon. When waves do develop, they cannot beat against any one section of shore for long. Movements of the tide continually cover or uncover the beach as waves roll in. In this way wave energy is distributed over a large vertical distance by the tide.

Most of the lower and middle bay shores are composed of resistant rock of molten origin, but the upper bay nestles in soft conglomerate, sandstone and shale. Exposed to water and winter temperatures, these rocks dissolve and crack easily, and even minor wave action will erode them. These are the rocks that have been sculpted into the bizarre Hopewell Cape "flowerpots" and the grottos, stacks, cliffs and sculptures of the park shoreline. In addition to the fast rate of erosion, land on the New Brunswick side of the bay is sinking at a rate of 30 cm per century, an aftereffect of glacial rebound. This brings waves closer to the base of cliffs year by year, allowing them to cut deeper and make the cliffs less stable. Yearly changes to weak sections of the shoreline can be noticed.

Rocks on Fundy's beaches have travelled there from a variety of sources. Some were carried far from their origin by glaciers and deposited nearby when the ice melted. Others have recently eroded from the andesite, sandstone or conglomerate cliffs of the park. Some washed down rivers from inland, were dumped at the river mouths, and are slowly migrating along the coast in the grip of currents. Perhaps the most fascinating are fragments of the original Appalachian mountains. Eroded and deposited more than 300 million years ago, they eventually solidified into red conglomerates. These are now being broken up into their components: pebbles of granite, basalt, porphyry, quartzite, jasper and other ancient mountain rocks. After a 300-million-year reprieve they now resume the process of erosion and deposition.

LIVING BY THE TIDES

Along the upper part of the beach, just out of the reach of waves, lives a special community of plants. Adapted to salt spray, exposure, drought and thin soil, they thrive where few other plants can even survive. Marram grass, beach-pea, sea rocket and dusty miller (or wormwood) reach their roots deep into the coarse sand, searching for fresh water and nutrients while holding the banks tightly in place. The heavy sands of the park beaches do not easily blow away but can be washed out when the bars are breached by storm waves.

On sections of rocky coast, the land's edge belongs to plants that can tolerate wind, cold, and occasional salt spray. Hugging the cliffsides are plants such as starry false Solomon's-seal, Laurentian primrose, green

PARKS CANADA

Seaweed-covered rocks, Herring Cove

alder, mountain ash, roseroot and a variety of grasses and lichens, including the almost fluorescent orange rock-encrusting *Xanthoria*. Just below the cliffs is a dark band of oily or sooty black lichens grazed by rough periwinkles.

On each beach, the last high tide is marked by a wrack line of sea-washed debris — crisp black bunches of dried seaweeds, feathers, frosted glass gems, fish bones, shells, driftwood carved and etched by decay, plastic artefacts, and objects rendered unidentifiable by the alchemy of sun, salt and surf. As tide height decreases with the approach of a neap tide, a whole series of wrack lines develops — black stripes parallel to the water's edge, each marking an earlier, slightly higher tide. After a storm, the wrack line is a tangle of fresh plants and animals washed up on the shore then deserted by the sea, a perfect place to start an exploration of the beach.

Boulders and cobbles below the wrack line support bright green seaweeds, called mermaid's hair, and tiny marine snails called rough periwinkles. Beneath rocks hide sideswimmers or scuds, small relatives of shrimp and lobsters that feed on washed-up debris. Lower down the beach, uncovered bit by bit by the receding water, slippery brown seaweeds called knotwrack and bladderwrack cling to the rocks.

Most exposed rock surfaces are covered with a yellow-white crust of barnacles. These lobster relatives live in shells permanently glued to rocks. Feeding only when the water covers them, they shelter beneath rock-hard trap doors that seal their protective "bunkers" when the tide falls. There they await the splash of waves that signals the rising tide, and food. Walking near a barnacle patch on a sunny day can elicit sounds rivaling those of the noisier breakfast cereals: hundreds of tiny trapdoors slam shut as the barnacles react to the passing shadows.

Knotwrack

Rock crab

PARKS CANADA

Dog whelks, barnacles and periwinkles: low tide (left); high tide (right)

At the same level as the sedentary barnacles are common periwinkles, grazers that feed on the fields of microscopic algae that coat each rock and plant in their tiny world. Snails' slime-trails catch particles from the water and trace each animal's movements in a muddy filigree. Fierce predators lurk here too. Large (3-cm-long), muscular dog whelks, the wolves of the marine forest, are able to rip the doors off a barnacle's stronghold, or to chase down, hold and breach the protective shell of a periwinkle. Whelks range over the boulders in search of prey and help to maintain a balance of species in the intertidal zone.

Most plants in this zone are rubbery, tough and flexible. Because they secrete a gelatinous slime, they can toss and twist and rub over each other as they move with the waves without abrading on sharp rocks or breaking apart.

The animals living here either take shelter under seaweed and rock when the tide falls or have thick protective shells with tight-fitting doors. The heat of day, dry air and even fresh rain water can be deadly to exposed sea animals, so they rely on their shells or rocks for shelter for as much as half of the day, between high tides. As the water rises, waves beat against the rocks, but the tough holdfasts of the seaweeds, the muscular feet of snails, and the glued shells of barnacles cling tightly enough to keep them from being torn loose and swept away.

Mud and gravel flats are home to an entirely different group of plants and animals. On the surface, under a thin film of water, live billions of microscopic algae that make food while the tide is low and stop when the muddy water rises over them. Hidden and sheltered in the mud are myriad worms of different shapes and sizes. Some form colonies, erecting tiny forests of glued-mud chimneys. When the tide rises they stick out feathery feeding tentacles to trap small plants and animals that wash by in the water. Others burrow actively just beneath the mud surface, preying on smaller, slower worms. Centimetre-long basketshell snails glide over the wet mud chasing down prey. Soft-shell clams hide beneath the beach surface, only the tips of their siphons showing as keyholes in the muddy gravel. Able to draw food and oxygen-laden water into their bodies through their siphons, clams have no need to forage, and lead sedentary lives. Their peace is sometimes disturbed by summer and winter storms, however, when entire beds are suffocated by thick blankets of shifting sediment. When the mud and gravel move again, clam graveyards are exposed, marked by scores of paired white shells, standing upright as they did in life, but empty.

Rocky depressions often act as tide pools, holding water throughout the low tide, allowing a wider range of living things to remain on the beach as the tide recedes. Seaweeds, such as Irish moss, kelp, colander wrack, corallina and encrusting red algae, cling to the rocks in these pools. Mussels live in cracks, small sea anemones wave stubby tentacles from the shelter of rocky shelves, tube worms poke feeding fans out of sandy tunnels between the rocks, and fish lie camouflaged on the bottom, trying to avoid predators. Some of the fish found in tide pools or hiding under moist rocks are butterfish or rock eels, tadpole-like juvenile lumpfish, young sculpins, and mottled young flounder. Some snail shells will suddenly sprout legs and wander around the pool bottom. These are empty shells that have been appropriated by hermit crabs for protection. Rock crabs and green crabs crouch under boulders, ever alert for dead fish, worms and other soft-bodied animals for food.

Other animals are left on the beaches by falling tides. Goosefish, also known as anglerfish and monkfish, grow to more than one metre long and have flat bodies, most of which is head. Most of the head is teeth. Each fish angles with a baited rod that protrudes from its forehead, drawing small fish close enough that when the goosefish quickly gapes its huge mouth, any nearby fish is vacuumed in. In the late summer, numbers of goosefish are stranded when they come inshore, perhaps to breed.

Squid, and their egg masses which resemble tangles of spotted gelatinous fingers, wash up on the beaches in late summer, as do dogfish — harmless metre-long sharks. Every now and then, something larger shows up, such as the harbour seal that was stuck on Alma Beach one low tide. It pretended to be a rock until the water returned and it could leave. Harbour seals and porpoises are seen offshore infrequently throughout the summer and autumn.

In April 1901, a 22-m finback whale washed ashore on Alma Beach. It was suggested at the time that it had been harpooned by a crew out of Hillsborough, and it was eventually flensed where it lay. Reports also state that the carcass was followed by a number of sharks, some up to 5 m long. Although present at the mouth of the bay, neither whales nor sharks are commonly seen in the upper bay today, and even in 1901 the occurrence excited sightseers. Stools made of whale backbone could be found in gardens around Alma for years afterwards.

To avoid their boats' being beached like the whale, the lobster and scallop fishermen who work out of Alma must come and go with the high tides. Lobsters are lured into baited wooden traps weighted with rocks or concrete slabs to hold them on the bottom of the bay. A long nylon line is attached to each trap, and a float at the top of the line marks its position. Up to 300 traps are set by each fisherman, and these must be hauled up, checked and rebaited every few days. This hauling and lowering of traps would not be too tedious in shallow water, but the traps are often set at depths of 40 m (22 fathoms) or more, and each must have about 120 m (66 fathoms) of line to keep its buoy above the water at high tide. Power winches help to haul the traps, and catches average 0.5 to 1.5 kg of lobster per trap. Bay of Fundy lobsters must weigh at least 0.5 kg to be legally caught; the largest trapped locally weighed 7.5 kg. Throughout the course of a year, there are two fishing seasons for lobster — 1 March to 31 July and 15 October to 31 December — though ice and cold make fishing impossible during parts of these periods. Between lobster seasons, scallops are dredged with a special wire mesh trawl. This drag is lowered onto a scallop bed and hauled along by boat. Once raised to the surface, scallops are picked out, and debris is thrown overboard. Some of the interesting non-commercial items brought up by scallop dredges are deep water animals such as sponges, sea squirts, sea cucumbers and even a few 10-cm-long octopuses.

At one time, fish weirs were in operation all around the bay. Now they are found mainly near its mouth. Weir fishing at the head of the bay was a form of fishing that required no boat. In fact, a fisherman could collect his catch with a horse and wagon. Tall poles were anchored in a heart shape on the bouldery beaches. The poles were strung with net that reached from their tops to just above the beach gravel. Woven around the bases of the poles was a screen of saplings. From the shore out to the trap stretched a wall of net or woven saplings that led fish into the trap as they swam along shore at high tide. Once they entered the weir, the incurving entrance kept fish swimming in circles as the tide dropped. Eventually, they were left high and dry, ready to be thrown into the back of a wagon. This strange form of fishing depended on high tides and a knowledge of fish movements. Now, weirs that once caught herring, shad, gaspareau (alewives), skate, sturgeon, pollock, salmon, flounder, dogfish and large numbers of other fish exist only as outlines of rocks and stubby posts on Alma and Cannontown beaches.

One of the few really dangerous organisms in this part of the country is a plant so small that it can not be seen without a microscope. This tiny, single-celled, gold-coloured alga, *Gonyaulax excavata,* floats with other plant and animal plankton in the surface waters of the bay. In the lower bay, summer and early autumn water conditions are often favourable for blooms — rapid increases in the numbers of these algae.

As the plants grow and multiply, each produces small amounts of chemicals within its body. Unfortunately, one of these natural chemicals is an extremely powerful nerve poison, which affects humans and other vertebrates as a sickness called paralytic shellfish poisoning (PSP). Some marine animals, including clams, mussels and scallops, feed by filtering tens of litres of water through their bodies each day and straining out microscopic particles of food. These shellfish concentrate poison from the thousands of algae they consume, but are themselves unharmed. Humans who have eaten as few as six clams from affected areas have died from the effects of the poison. Severe discomfort is a more common result with numbness, nausea, headache and paralysis sometimes lasting for days.

For unknown reasons, the funnel-like lower Bay of Fundy and the mouth of the St. Lawrence River seem particularly prone to the development of PSP. Shellfish are tested throughout the summer by public health officials, and affected beaches are posted with signs that warn of the danger. It is illegal to collect shellfish from a posted area. All commercially collected and prepared shellfish must come from safe beaches. If you intend to gather your own shellfish, check with local authorities. The heat of cooking decreases the toxicity of affected shellfish, and some people seem more resistant than others, but why take chances? Red tides are caused by related organisms and occur along both coasts of North America. Watch at night for bioluminescence, a greenish light that shows in the wake of boats, and waves breaking on a beach. This phenomenon is occasionally caused by the same tiny plants.

This bay of the giant tides has given the park its name and character, and fascinates visitors above all other attractions that the park can offer. No visit is complete without a walk to the edge of the low tide — a walk on the bottom of the sea.

FOREST OF DARKNESS, FOREST OF LIGHT

Most of the tall trees are gone now. Once, the Acadian Forest of New Brunswick, Nova Scotia and parts of Maine was a dense patchwork of different-aged trees. A transition zone between the hardwood-rich forests of the Great Lakes–Saint Lawrence Forest Region and the conifers of the Boreal Forest Region, the Acadian Forest shared the characteristic species of both. Throughout the province, elm, silver maple, ash, butternut, hemlock and basswood grew in deep river valley soils. Where fires had burned, the forests were composed of fast-growing hardwoods and jack pine. In wet, boggy soils, black spruce and larch thrived, and along the moist, relatively fire-free coast of the Bay of Fundy rose a dense forest of red spruce, balsam fir, white and yellow birch, and maple.

With the rapid influx of Europeans to New Brunswick in the late 1700s, trees around growing towns like Saint John were felled to build houses and boats and for export to seemingly insatiable markets in the United States and Europe. Settlers cleared their land with axe and fire, levelling many thousands of square kilometres of forest. As fast as new trees grew they were removed, at first for lumber, later for pulp. Steadily the standards for minimum harvestable tree size dropped. Even within Fundy National Park, after its establishment in 1948, the cutting continued, though at a much reduced rate. Large timbers were needed for the reconstruction of the Fortress of Louisbourg, a National Historic Park, and until 1965, spruce were felled for this purpose in the Bennett Lake area.

Near Herring Cove and along the banks of Rossiter and Hawkes brooks and at a few other places in the park are remnants of older forest. Perhaps because of their inaccessibility they survived, or were cut so long ago that all signs of disturbance have healed. These small stands probably resemble the forest that the first settlers found here in the early 1800s, a forest that once stretched across the province.

Cutting is no longer allowed within the park, save for the clearing of trails and the removal of deadfalls from roads and campgrounds; still, for the most part the tall trees have vanished.

SPRUCE BUDWORM, AGENT OF CHANGE

In the aftermath of lumbering, dense masses of fast-growing balsam fir sprouted in the shallow, acidic soils. As these trees reached a crowded maturity and were ready to set seed, they were set upon by a small brown forest moth called the spruce budworm. Little notice had been paid to this insect since it preferred to feed on balsam fir, long considered a weak and useless weed tree. Caterpillars of the budworm fed on fir and spruce needles, and multiplied until the situation reached epidemic proportions. Province-wide, vast stands of fir fed increasing hordes of these insects. By the late 1940s, balsam fir was required in large quantities by the New Brunswick forest industry for pulp production. Private pulp and paper interests were given the upper hand in the battle for the trees in 1952 when aerially applied insecticides began to be used by the province. Annual spraying continues to this day. Fundy National Park was sprayed from 1969 to 1975, at which time it was decided to let the budworms run their natural course within the park's boundaries. Over the last fifteen years, about one-third of the park has been defoliated, but now the situation seems to have stabilized, and forest stands are regenerating.

Like moose and beaver, spruce budworm are native to this continent and have probably been eating fir and spruce needles for as long as there has been an Acadian Forest. Where the insects were most abundant, nearly all of the trees have been killed. The forest, however, lives on. Dead trees provide food for wood-rotting fungi. Carpenter ants and beetle larvae feed in the decomposing wood; woodpeckers dig in the softening trees for insects and raise their young in nests chiselled out of the decaying trunks.

Standing dead trees festooned with old man's beard and other lichens become veritable hanging gardens of tiny plants. Lichens are neither harmful nor helpful to the trees on which they grow, and only use the branches and trunks for support, as hats hang on a hat-rack. They obtain most of their nutrients from fog and rain and the mineral and organic substances dissolved in them. As many as 30 different species of lichens can grow on one tree, each in its own special niche. Others carpet the forest floor, coat rocks and, in effect, colonize anything that does not move, from the edge of the tide to the top of the highest peak. A recent survey of Fundy National Park found 431 species of lichens, and there are probably more yet to be identified.

With the needles gone from budworm-killed trees, more sunlight reaches the forest floor, encouraging a flush of shrubs and small trees. Hectares of raspberries and yellow and white birch saplings have shot up from rhizomes and seeds long-buried in the soil. Some of the young hardwoods have grown more than 4 m tall in the last decade. Small spruce and fir, dwarfed for years by the shade of mature trees, have been released from the dark and are forming dense stands — prime material for thinning by local porcupines. Mature trees are out of reach as winter food for deer, moose and hare; the new growth, however, is at just the right height for browsing.

Most attractive to budworm, and less able to withstand the effects of defoliation, balsam fir was hit hardest by the insect. With the dying-off of fir trees, budworm numbers declined, and spruce trees have started to recover. Bumper cone crops have been produced in recent years, and red squirrels, uncommon in the park while the trees were weak, are once again seen and heard almost everywhere. Piles of cones and empty cone-scales litter stumps where squirrels have fed, and the animals' squeaky chatter scolds intruders.

Budworm will be a part of this forest for as long as fir and spruce grow in Fundy. Occasional changes in budworm numbers, or in such organisms as the balsam woolly aphid, forest tent caterpillar, and other forest insects and fungi will continue to throw the forest into dramatic change. A healthy forest cannot exist without the deaths of some of the plants and animals within it. The nutrients that a tree takes from the shallow soil are locked up in its wood for decades, unavailable to most other growing things. Through the recycling of old trees, nutrients are made available again, and the continuity of the forest is ensured. Fire is rare along the bayshore, so the spruce budworm is the principal agent of recycling in Fundy's forests.

In many places, hardwood forest is replacing the original groves of spruce and fir. The fast growth of birch throughout the budworm-killed stands is probably due to the weakening of conifers before they finally succumbed. Hard hit by the insects, the conifers did not have the energy to produce seeds. Birches, on the other hand, had no such problems, and year after year poured out seeds. With the death of the fir and spruce a new forest of birch has sprung up. Yet even now, growing slowly in the shade of the hardwoods, small balsam fir and red spruce await their moment in the sun. The spruce-fir forest will return to Fundy's hills.

IN THE SHADE OF THE CONIFERS

Throughout the year the floor of a healthy spruce-fir forest is in dense shade, and only a few specialized plants can survive there. Ferns and mosses grow in the moist acid soil, surrounded by dead needles, twigs and fallen cones. Only where a tree has died does much light penetrate the canopy, releasing a flush of growth until the clearing is once again filled.

Few large animals live here since most of the food is high out of reach. Once, mature coniferous forest was the home of woodland caribou. They fed mostly on the lichens that draped tree trunks and branches and covered bare soil and rock, places in which moose and deer could not thrive.

Where light mottles the ground, shade-tolerant plants creep over fallen trees and form a green carpet. Bunchberry, wild sarsaparilla, wood sorrel, clintonia lily, goldthread, maianthemum, creeping snowberry and twinflower form small clumps or completely cover the soil. Flowering in masses at different times during the late spring and summer they add colour to the darkness of the woods. Sprouting from the ground in deeper shade are cushion moss, feather moss, leafy liverworts, haircap moss and, in moist hollows, sphagnum or peat moss. In midsummer, ghostly white clumps of Indian pipe burst from the soil like malformed mushrooms. These are true flowering plants that have lost the ability to use sunlight to make food. Lacking chlorophyll, they depend on a relationship with wood- and leaf-rotting fungi to survive.

Spruce, fir, pine and other conifers do lose their needle-like leaves, but unlike the hardwoods, they do not lose them all at once. Larches are the exception, blazing golden yellow in the late autumn, just before they are denuded by wind and rain. Other conifers will retain individual needles for three to eleven years, losing them a few at a time as they wear out. When an entire spruce or fir turns brown and dumps its needles, it is usually a sign that a hungry porcupine has girdled the bark and killed the tree.

Balsam fir trees sometimes have dense nest-like clusters of twigs in their upper branches. These "witches' brooms" are caused by a fungus that produces chemicals similar to the tree's own growth hormones. Instead of one twig on a branch growing longer than all of the others, each twig on an infected branch grows rapidly, forming a broom. When mature, the broom is covered with clumps of yellow spores produced by the fungus. Witches' brooms slow the growth of a tree but rarely kill it.

THE HARDWOOD FOREST — SPRING FLOWERS AND SUMMER SHADOWS

Most plants of the forest floor must flower and set seed before the trees leaf out. Their life cycles are compressed into the very short productive period between snowmelt and the shade of summer. In this respect, they share the timing problems that face plants of the Arctic and of deserts. While snow still lingers in the valleys where conifers predominate, the floor of the hardwood forest bursts with unfurling leaves, pushed up through the leaf and branch litter that mulched them throughout the winter. In the space of a few weeks, millions of flowers will open to blanket the sun-dappled forest floor. Insects, slow in the cool spring air, bumble from flower to flower pollinating as they feed. Trout lily, Dutchman's breeches, rose twisted-stalk, spring beauty and purple trillium mix with the fronds of shade-loving ferns. Soon the flowers set seed and the plants quickly die

Purple trillium

Wood sorrel

Bunchberry

back to the protection of the leaf mould, just as sunlight is obscured by a canopy of tree leaves and fern fronds. Within a couple of weeks, nothing remains to betray the presence of these ephemeral flowers as they wait beneath the soil for signs of the next spring.

During the summer, broad leaves shade the forest floor, and as in the spruce-fir forest, few plants can grow. Verdant wood ferns and maple seedlings break the uniformity of a hardwood forest floor that is brown with the leaves of previous summers. Dead leaves act not only as a protective winter blanket for established plants but also as a barrier which prevents many seeds from rooting. Few mosses grow here, for they are too quickly smothered by leaf litter.

Yellow birch trees are normally the largest trees in hardwood stands, attaining greater girths than the surrounding sugar maples and beech. In many cases, the tops of the birches are dead, and an umbrella of branches sprouts from beneath the rotting crown. In New Brunswick, this tree is near the northern limit of its range and is probably more susceptible to damage because of this stress. About forty-five years ago, a condition known as birch dieback began to affect white and yellow birch, hitting the latter most severely. Death of the crown and often of the entire tree resulted. The cause is still unknown. Whether it was a disease or an environmental change, the effects of the dieback live on in the parasol-shaped survivors.

That yellow birch trees cling tenaciously to life is evident along most trails. Living birches with dead crowns have suffered badly from rot. Water and fungi can enter through an exposed dead top, turning the centre of the trunk into a crumbling pulp. In many cases, a living shell still grows around this rotten wood, and the tree looks normal. Damage to the bark by porcupines, abrasion or disease stimulates rooting in the branches above, causing a tree to send thick roots reaching for the soil down through its own rotting trunk. As the punky wood falls away, these roots stand like spindly stems, clustered together, straining to keep the remaining crown upright. Some yellow birch have survived for decades in this precarious state.

Yellow birch wood is usually easy to recognize, even when well rotted or washed up on a riverbank or beach. Distinct ripples mark the wood, resembling wavy blond hair. A live tree can be identified by its yellowish, flaky bark and the wintergreen fragrance released from twigs when scratched. The roots of yellow birch, red spruce and some other trees occasionally graft with those of neighbours of the same species. In this way, whole stands of trees may be linked beneath the soil. Grafts are often exposed where a trail passes through the forest, and the soil is compacted.

American beech were once important trees on well-drained, rocky soils in southern New Brunswick. Since the thirties, however, disease has reduced them to contorted, shrubby monsters. *Nectria,* the fungus that causes beech bark canker, was accidentally introduced to North America from Europe. It is unwittingly aided in its invasion of healthy trees by the beech scale insect, which bores tiny holes in the trees' protective bark while feeding. Instead of growing thick straight trunks with velvet-smooth grey bark, infected beech trees stay small and spindly and have pitted and scarred trunks. Mosses and lichens cling to the holes, decorating them with fringes that accentuate the grotesque malformation. Few beechnuts fall to the ground now, for the trees are too stressed to produce them.

Unhealthy though they are, beech still sprout their soft copper-coloured leaves every spring, each glistening under a coat of fine silvery hairs. The dark glossy leaves, stirred by summer breezes, rustle and flutter. Gold in autumn, then brown, beech leaves cling to the trees throughout the winter, rattling and clattering, brittle in the cold air. Like yellow birch, beech are survivors.

Autumn brings colour to the hardwood forest. At first, only a few early trees glow red against the background of green. By the middle of October, shades of yellow, gold, red and orange shine from every patch of hardwoods, and hillsides glow in kaleidoscopic splendour. Within a few weeks the spectacle is over. Dead brown leaves litter the ground and grey branches rake the cold white sky as the monochrome of winter descends.

LIFE IN THE ACADIAN FOREST

Mixed forest covers the largest portion of the park. Here, conifers and hardwoods intermingle, and on the forest floor grow plants that are characteristic of both coniferous and deciduous forests.

Painted trillium and hobblebush (moosewood) prefer this sort of forest, as does the pink lady's slipper orchid. Creamy white lady's slippers, a northern form of the same plant, are frequently seen in the park. Clubmosses, or lycopods, form dense rings or streamers of dark evergreen growth. Ground pine, ground cedar, shining clubmoss, bristly clubmoss and other species trail through the trees, spreading slightly year by year. Late each summer their yellow reproductive cones shed clouds of spores on each dry breeze.

In many places, fern glades form large clearings. Where trees have fallen and hay-scented fern, wood fern and bracken have become firmly established, the solid mass of fronds seems to prevent young trees from growing. Whether caused by shade or by chemicals produced by the ferns, these treeless glades provide a bright counterpoint to the shade of forest trails.

Conifers often have only shallow "plate" roots, and strong winter winds can knock over exposed trees. Hardwood trees are far less prone to winter windthrow than conifers, since their bare branches offer less surface area. Ice storms, however, do take their toll on hardwoods. As ice builds on the branches of conifers they droop with the weight, but since they usually jut at right angles from the tree trunk, they do not bend far enough to break. The upright branches of hardwoods, especially of white birch, bend then snap, sometimes leaving whole stands of trees topless.

When a large tree falls, it does not take long for decomposition to start. Often fungi and carpenter ants have begun to work before the tree is toppled. The honey mushroom (*Armilariella*) causes root rot that weakens and kills conifers, and its bootlace-like threads can sometimes be seen glowing at night from fallen trunks. Mosses and lichens coat the bark, sealing in moisture that promotes the growth of fungi and bacteria. Orange blobs of jelly-textured witches' butter fungus glisten from broken ends of

Clockwise from top left: chanterelle; scabrous leccinum; showy hygrophorus; witches' butter

logs. Soon dead wood softens, turning papery, pulpy or crumbly, depending on its moisture content and what is rotting it. Mineral soil, laid bare as a tree falls and its roots tear loose of the earth, is a ready-made seed bed for young conifers, and the extra light that reaches the forest floor spurs their growth.

Hardwood seedlings sprout in the deep moist soil provided by the decomposing nurse log. In a few decades, a row of mature trees will be the only clue to the position of the original trunk. Some of these will have stilt-like roots supporting their trunks well off the ground, a sign that they grew atop a log which then rotted and fell away.

Many forest fungi are necessary for the healthy growth of trees. Growing closely around or into the surface of developing roots, the fungi remove from the trees substances, such as vitamins, that they cannot produce on their own. Trees in turn benefit from moisture and nutrients that fungi can gather more effectively. Since fungi spread over large areas beneath the soil surface and can decompose dead plant matter, they form an important food network which trees and other plants can tap into. An impression of the actual size of a forest fungus plant can be gained by comparing their fruit — mushrooms — to apples on an apple tree. In the case of the fungus, only the mushroom (the "apple") is visible above ground; the bulk of the plant (the "tree") spreads underground through the leaf mould, sometimes covering hundreds of square metres.

Forest composed mainly of spruce and fir tends to dominate moist, cool sites within the park, while well-drained south-facing hills are invariably mantled with hardwoods. A few white pine cling to dry ridge tops, but they are rare. Peculiarly, red pine, elm, eastern white cedar, larch, hemlock, oak and ash are almost unrepresented in the park, though they grow commonly in the surrounding area. Poplar and cherry are uncommon in the park, and jack pine is absent, probably because of the lack of frequent fires that promote the spread of these trees.

In time, the small patch of New Brunswick forest that is Fundy National Park will assume greater and greater importance. Forests throughout eastern Canada are rapidly being harvested and becoming ever more intensively managed, perhaps to the point that they will eventually be tree farms rather than forests.

THE ANIMAL SHOW

A movement caught by the corner of an eye; a rustle, a rushing, a cry; prints in the soft soil; trails in the snow; sights, signs and sounds. Without them, a park visit would feel incomplete; without them the forest would seem empty. Everyone wants to see animals, and few visitors leave Fundy National Park disappointed.

Silence, care and patience are three traits required for animal-watching. Luck is the important fourth. With these, it is possible to approach even the wariest deer or the shyest bird for a photograph.

Most numerous and least understood of the park's wildlife are the worms, insects, spiders and other small creepers and crawlers, the "invertebrates" (animals without backbones). For some reason, many humans are deathly afraid of these tiny and fragile animals. They are, for the most part, far less dangerous to us than we are to them.

Insects

The largest group of invertebrates are the insects, and of them, our attention is most often caught by those colourful fliers, the butterflies. They careen from flower to flower, congregating at those particularly attractive to them, such as joe-pye weed, goldenrod and thistle, or along roadsides and river banks where they gather en masse to lick up mineral salts that have dried on the gravel. The colours of summer butterflies are a forerunner of autumn's golds, reds and oranges, and are a shimmering reward after the sober browns, greys and white of the long winter months. Frequently seen butterflies are the tiger swallowtail, white admiral, red admiral, morning cloak, the tiny coppers, skippers and blues, and the orange fritillaries. The great spangled fritillary is very common in the park throughout the summer. Its caterpillars feed on the leaves of violets.

Dragonflies, darters and damselflies skim low over the waters of ponds and riversides, rustling as they fly, their wings shimmering like cut glass in the sunlight. These flying predators chase down and capture their prey on the wing, as their giant ancestors did over 300 million years ago. They feed on smaller flying insects and sometimes hover close to people, watching for unwary mosquitos and blackflies. Even though they are often referred to as "devil's darning needles," dragonflies are harmless, and are too beautiful and graceful to deserve this slander.

As night falls, moths start to appear. Most spectacular are the cecropia, polyphemus and luna moths — large native silk moths, which can attain wing spans of 15 cm, and fly more like birds than insects. Unfortunately, their colours — the luna's lime green, the others' reds, yellows and browns — are rarely seen since these moths fly only after dark.

Amphibians

Spring and early summer nights vibrate with the mating calls of frogs and toads. The earliest performers are the clucking wood frogs and the tiny spring peepers whose forceful whistles echo in shrill massed chorus across the dark ponds. These sounds are soon augmented by the long trills of toads. Marshy ponds and lakes are the homes of leopard and pickerel frogs whose roars and growls mix with the "plunks" of green frogs, and — later in the summer — the bass droning roar of bullfrogs.

Salamanders, the park's other amphibians, are mute. Six species live in moist places: the spotted, red-backed and four-toed in mossy glades and inside rotten logs; the dusky and two-lined under rocks near springs and brooks, and adult spotted newts in ponds and lakes. Four-toed salamanders have not been found anywhere else in New Brunswick, and Fundy is the only Canadian national park known to contain dusky salamanders.

Reptiles

Although wild snapping turtles and wood tortoises are found close to the park, only a handful of the latter have actually been seen inside its boundaries, and are presumed to have been pets released by visitors. The park's rugged terrain and the rocky and boggy characteristics of its lakes make the establishment of a breeding colony of these reptiles unlikely.

There are no naturally occurring poisonous snakes in the park, in New Brunswick, or anywhere in the Atlantic Provinces. The largest and most common park reptile is the eastern garter snake. Up to a metre long, garter snakes feed on larger prey than do other indigenous snakes, catching small mammals, frogs, young birds and insects. The larger ones will try to bite when handled. Their hundreds of tiny, needle-like teeth can pierce the skin and sometimes snap off. Some people react to the bite of garter snakes, but to most of us they are harmless. Like most other snakes, their main defence is to stay still and try to avoid detection, and to flee if approached too closely. When caught, they excrete a strong musky paste from their vents, which is most effective in securing their release.

Green snakes — emerald above and cream-coloured below — grow to about 50 cm long. Like the smaller red-bellied snake, they are most often found in old fields and around rock piles. Both feed mainly on insects. The

Polyphemus moth   *Eastern garter snake*

ring-necked snake is uncommon. It only grows to 30 cm long, and feeds at night on insects and salamanders.

Birds

After winter's snow has melted, but before leaves are on the trees, the birds arrive. Moving up the bay from southern wintering grounds, flock after flock of migrants swarm northward to summer nesting grounds. Robins and grackles, blackbirds and cowbirds, sparrows and finches, warblers and swallows arrive in waves. Noisy, colourful and very hungry, they alight and search for food, often becoming so engrossed that they seem not to notice birdwatchers only an arm's length away. After feeding, some stay and set up territories in nesting areas, but many continue their journey northward.

Birds that stay throughout the winter take advantage of any food that is available. Seeds, dried berries and apples, hibernating insects, buds and scraps of flesh and fat from dead animals, all enter the diet of birds that must survive the long cold. For this reason a resident bird must be a jack-of-all-trades. No hummingbirds or ant-eating flickers, no wading birds or eaters of freshwater fish, and no insect-catching swallows or warblers could live long past the first snowfall. They move south to gentler climes; only the hardy remain.

Ravens, bluejays, gray jays, hairy and downy woodpeckers, golden-crowned kinglets, nuthatches, brown creepers, black-capped and boreal chickadees, tree sparrows, juncos, white-winged crossbills, ruffed grouse and a few evening grosbeaks are the most common winter residents of Fundy's forest.

Ruffed grouse, the size of small chickens, raise large broods each year. A pattern of brown and grey feathers provides protective camouflage, and like the hare, grouse use slow movements and silence to avoid detection. Early spring resonates with deep throbbing sounds as males drum for the attention of females. During the next few weeks, the female broods her eggs. As soon as the chicks have hatched out, they are able to walk and feed, and the nest is abandoned. An amble through the forest at this time of year will often bring you near a grouse and her brood, and she will try to warn you away with cat-like mews and hisses. The chicks stay hidden and stock-still until the female signals to gather them. If she is really upset by your presence, she may even try to scare you by charging. As comical as it may seem to be chased away by a spitting-mad bird, it is best to retreat and let her lead her chicks to safety. If you press on, the young could scatter and be lost.

In the autumn, grouse remain together as a family, and if survival has been good, groups of a dozen or more birds will feed and roost in one place. One of life's biggest thrills can come from walking unwittingly into a covey of these birds. They stay quiet until you get just a little too close. In one heart-jolting second the silence of the forest is rent by an explosion of wings and flying objects. All around you, large grey *things* hurtle into trees, crash through branches, and disappear noisily into the undergrowth. You and your heart are left to recover in silence.

Hawks and owls cruise these fields for food: kestrels, redtailed hawks, broad-winged hawks and the occasional harrier. Some prefer open fields, others forest edges. The goshawk and sharp-shinned hawk patrol deep woods. Each is adapted to hunt a certain kind of prey in a specific habitat. The nightshift of flying predators includes the great horned owl, long-eared owl, barred owl and the tiny saw-whet. Most commonly heard but rarely visible are great horned and barred owls. They are inquisitive and will answer a human's hoots. Flying soundlessly from tree to tree, a single hooting bird can give you the impression that you are surrounded by owls.

Mammals

Moose are the largest of Fundy's mammals, weighing over half a tonne. There are about thirty of them in the park, and most live in the uplands, feeding near bogs and lakes. White-tail deer stay mainly in the more open coastal area and feed in fields and along roadsides. The park deer population is somewhere between 300 and 400. These two mammals could live together in the same area quite peacefully except for a third animal, a tiny hair-like nematode, or roundworm, with a name bigger than it is — *Parelaphostrongylus tenuis*. This worm lives quite harmlessly in the brains of deer, which seem to have adapted to it over thousands of years. At one stage in its life-cycle, however, the nematode sheds masses of eggs which travel through the deer's body, hatch and end up as larvae in the infected deer's intestines. The larvae are left on the ground in piles of droppings.

MICHAEL BURZYNSKI

White-tail buck

Slugs and snails crawl around the droppings and are penetrated by the parasite larvae. Under the control of the parasites, infected snails and slugs seem to lose their instinct to hide during the day, and stay in the open on grass and branches. There they are accidentally consumed by browsing deer which are then infected, completing the cycle. If moose feed in the same area, they too may become infected, and often suffer grievous consequences. Instead of a benign infection, the worms move from the intestines of the moose into its spine. From there they migrate to the lining of the brain where they can cause bleeding and swelling, and the fate of the moose is sealed.

First, eyesight and hearing are affected, then balance. Unable to feed or drink, and standing with difficulty, the moose slowly dies. The effects of the brainworm make infected moose appear dazed. They stagger about, approaching people and cars without fear, eyes lolling, tongue hanging loose; a dying moose is a sorry sight. Unfortunately, nothing can be done to save a sick animal, and no immunization exists for those yet uninfected. What saves most moose is the difference in habitat requirements between them and deer. Perhaps some day the survivors will adapt to the presence of this tiny parasite, but until then we will continue to lose a few animals each year.

MICHAEL BURZYNSKI

Groundhogs

Mild coastal weather leads to partial melting of snow at various times throughout each winter. As snow alternately melts and refreezes it forms a crust, sometimes thick enough to support an animal, sometimes not. Deep snow and the formation of thin, razor-sharp crusts hinder the movement of large mammals such as deer. Moose are somewhat better off; their long legs allow them to wade through snow almost as easily as they do through water, and their wide hoofs distribute their weight. They will gather in yards only during exceptionally difficult winters. Deer have shorter legs and narrow hoofs. Only by herding in areas with a good food supply and trampling the snow into a series of paths can they survive harsh winters. From a sheltered central resting area, their hard-packed trails radiate in a spidery network. From these, deer lunge through deep snow to reach the tender twigs on which they subsist during the winter.

There have been as many as twenty-five active beaver colonies in the park at a time, though most years the number is closer to ten. Dams are easily built in the deep, narrow river valleys, and they can quickly back up a lot of water. The only problem is that the valley sides are covered with softwoods, and beavers prefer to feed on the tender twigs, leaves and underbark of hardwood trees. Unfortunately, in Fundy, hardwood trees usually grow on hilltops, out of the animals' reach. Also, the soil is too rocky and the hills too steep for them to build canals to these food sources.

Consequently, beavers tend to be transient, building a dam in an area and living there for a few years, feeding on young hardwoods as fast as they sprout and even on raspberry canes. But soon the available food supply is exhausted and they are forced to move. Some small valleys, such as Hueston Brook, are jammed with the relics of old dams, lodges and overgrown ponds.

Varying, or snowshoe, hares are seen more often than any park mammal except deer. Named for their changeable coats — brown in summer, white in winter — and their huge hind feet, which act as snowshoes, these hares are found everywhere. Favourite browsing sites are along roadsides and trails, in old fields and campgrounds, and in groves of small trees. When approached, a hare will sit motionless in an attempt to avoid detection, then dart away to better cover. Many hares carry passengers. Clinging to their ears and other patches of exposed skin are ticks that hitch a ride and extract a meal. Some become grossly engorged before dropping off to lay eggs. These ticks do not bite humans; perhaps they find us too gamy.

Old fields that have grown up in grasses, alders and spruce become excellent feeding grounds for deer and hare, and offer nesting sites for birds and small mammals. A rich food source such as this does not long go unexploited. Bobcats are rarely seen but common predators of small animals, and will even take the occasional fawn. Their droppings can sometimes be found along the Matthews Head Trail and on other grassy roadways in the park. Coyotes also feed in the fields, eating anything from bird eggs to carrion to berries. Red foxes prefer grassy open country, frequently haunting old fields and roadsides. They are wary of people and not often seen.

Squeaks and rustles betray the movements of the smaller mammals. Mice and shrews race through grassy tunnels and among tree roots, the mice in search of roots, leaves and berries, the shrews pursuing the mice. They zip across trails as grey blurs, rarely identifiable in their haste. Prey to all predators, their lives are short but productive. Some will have four litters in the course of a summer.

Although the greatest concentration of groundhogs is on the golf course, they seem to live anywhere there is enough soil for a tunnel. Their dens have been found in old fields, atop rocky cliffs, in the sandy dune beside Alma marsh and in the depths of Kinnie Brook valley. Surprising to many people is their habit of climbing bushes and small trees to nibble on buds in the spring. They clamber around like overweight squirrels, and emit piercing whistles when annoyed. Like deer and hare, groundhogs have benefited from the opening of the forest by man.

Striped skunks are not common in the park; only a handful have been seen in the last decade. Raccoons, however, are very numerous and can be a nuisance in campgrounds. They grow large (up to 9 kg), and their sharp

MICHAEL BURZYNSKI

Coyote

teeth can do a lot of damage to the hand that tries to feed them. Remember — it is illegal to feed wildlife in a national park.

Raccoons that become used to handouts are a definite problem and become quite belligerent towards anyone who does not oblige their appetites. Muggings by gangs of raccoons may sound unlikely but have occurred. When raccoons turn to crime and chance upon a picnic cooler of food left out at night, they will not hesitate to break in and steal the contents. They often fight over a choice morsel, growling, and tussling until the entire campsite is awake. Remember that there is only a thin canvas wall between you and whatever is out there.

The best way to avoid this sort of trouble is to obey the rules: feed only yourself and the blackflies (which help themselves), and keep your campsite clear of food and garbage.

Raccoons den along the coast between Headquarters and Herring Cove. Small caves and deep cracks riddle the crevassed sandstones in the Devil's Half Acre area and provide excellent wintering dens. Scores of raccoons gather in and around this area each year.

Dense stands of young spruce and fir, fields of tender grasses and herbs, and succulent maple, poplar and birch — these are the favourite foods of porcupines. During the winter they den in caves, hollow trees and under upturned roots, making forays into patches of young conifers when hungry. There they climb a tree and chew away the outer bark until the soft inner bark, or cambium, is exposed. Rich in sugars and vitamins, cambium provides them with a woody but nourishing diet. When spring

Raccoon

exposes the growing tips of grasses and field flowers, porcupines just waddle through the fields, grazing as they go. A porcupine is a fussy eater and will take sample bites from the bases of a number of trees until it finds one that suits it. It will then return to that tree, often a hardwood, until the bark is almost gone. Sometimes a tree is found that has been fed on for a number of years, and the layers of chewed wood, scars and healed-over wounds tell a story of attack and survival. However, once its bark is completely girdled, a tree dies.

Porcupines do an important pruning job on young trees. Since they feed on some trees but leave others of the same kind alone, they can quickly thin a stand. This allows a few trees to grow to maturity where before dozens struggled for survival. Like many forest mammals, porcupines will chew on bones and shed antlers to obtain the calcium and potassium not readily available in their food. For this reason animal remains are rarely found in the forest.

A porcupine's main defence is its quills — stiff, hollow, pointed hairs that are only loosely attached to the skin. When threatened, porcupines turn their backs to the danger and erect their quills. This makes the animal look twice as big, and exposes the quills' black-and-white warning pattern. If an aggressive coyote, bobcat or fisher gets too close, the porcupine will slap it with its muscular, quill-laden tail, driving spines deep into the aggressor's muzzle. While the wounded animal tries to shake loose its unwanted quill moustache, the porcupine beats a hasty retreat to the nearest tree. Quills work their way deeper and deeper into flesh, and can be fatal, though most eventually work loose. A porcupine's long heavy claws are used only for climbing.

Porcupines can not shoot their quills, and are not at all dangerous to people who keep their distance. Unfortunately, the defence posture adopted by the porcupine — back towards danger, quills raised — is not effective against cars. Please drive carefully and give these slow-moving animals lots of room.

The porcupine's major predator is the fisher, a dark, fox-sized member of the weasel family, once almost extinct in New Brunswick. A provincial reintroduction program began in 1966, and fishers were released just north of the park. Despite their name, these animals spend most of their time on the forest floor and in trees; they feed on voles, squirrels, hares, porcupines, birds, berries and carrion. Their ability to speedily flip over a porcupine and attack its unprotected belly is appreciated by foresters. Large populations of porcupines can clear their way methodically through tree plantations, and this is probably what led to the fisher reintroduction program.

Secretive, and good swimmers, these mammals are active day or night and, unlike the closely related marten, they will live in hardwood and mixed forests, old burns and immature forests. Man is their only important predator. Seen infrequently in the park, fishers most often betray their presence by tracks, by the "unzipped" remains of porcupines and by their quill-packed droppings. On viewing the latter, you may get the feeling that there must be an easier way to get a meal.

A few black bears regularly use the park area; normally shy, they are seen very rarely. Moving in and out as different foods become available during the growing season, they feed on grubs, vegetation, small mammals and berries. In blueberry season they graze berries and leaves from the low bushes. When raspberries ripen they sit in berry patches and gather armloads of canes to themselves, then pick off the berries with their lips. Swaths of flattened raspberry canes show where they have fed. Only occasionally do they venture into the campgrounds, lured by the smell of carelessly stored food or garbage. Unlike raccoons, bears will not fiddle with the catches of coolers, but just demolish them, take what they want and amble off into the forest. Please do not encourage bears, but do not try to stop them either. Always give bears a wide berth.

Known in the east as panther, painter, catamount and Indian devil, in the southwest as puma, and in the northwest as mountain lion or cougar, the largest North American member of the cat family lives on in New Brunswick. Once the most widespread mammal in the Americas, the panther or cougar has been squeezed into a few remaining wild places. Weighing from 35 to 70 kg and measuring up to 2 m in length (almost half of that tail), panthers prefer deer as prey, and range over huge territories while hunting. The eastern panther was considered extinct in New Brunswick after the last one was shot in 1932. Over the years since then, however, scores of sightings of large tawny or black cats have filtered in from around the province, many from the area of Fundy National Park. No photographs have been taken, only descriptions and track-casts, but the evidence seems to show that this ghost of the eastern forest still lives. One or two reliable reports of these cats reach park wardens each year, most-often describing brief roadside sightings of a strange large animal that suddenly appears then seems to dissolve into the trees.

Your chances of seeing a panther, even for a second, are extremely slim. Few park staff have ever had the pleasure of viewing one of these impressive wild lions, but the hope is there. If you do sight one, please inform a park warden as soon as possible.

Since the 1950s, coyotes have been introducing themselves to New Brunswick. Moving in from Maine and Quebec, they spread throughout the province, arriving at Fundy in 1978. Almost the same size as the extinct eastern timber wolf, coyotes seem to be filling the same niche in the food chain. Hares, mice and other small mammals, along with carrion, birds, insects, vegetation and the occasional fresh deer make up the coyotes' diet. Hunting alone or in small family groups, they scavenge in the old fields and along roadsides. Their nighttime sing-alongs may at first chill you to the bone, but after a while individual voices become recognizable and you may be tempted to join in.

Unless you are very, very small and habitually wear rabbit-fur coats while hiking, coyotes pose you no danger. They are about the size of a border collie and weigh an average of 15 kg. They are so wary of humans that you will be very lucky indeed to see one, even though you may hear them frequently. About twenty of these animals live in the park, as loners and in small family groups. Continuing study of coyotes will show how they interact with other animals in the park, both prey and predators, how far they range for food, and how their numbers increase and decrease with changing conditions.

It is, of course, illegal to hunt or trap in a national park. Feeding animals is also illegal, since it encourages bad habits and hygiene, and being on too intimate terms can be dangerous to both parties. Even the catching and handling of animals is detrimental to both the animals and their handlers. Small animals such as insects, frogs and salamanders can be injured by even the gentlest treatment, or poisoned by insect-repellent-covered hands. Others are large enough to try to defend themselves with claws, teeth, spines and other means. National parks exist to protect wildlife and habitat. As a visitor you may watch and photograph animals, but you must not feed them, disturb them or remove them from the park — by law.

REINTRODUCTIONS ALL AROUND

More than 350 years ago an aggressive new animal extended its range into eastern North America. An efficient large predator, it required an ever-increasing territory from which to obtain food and other resources. From a handful of initial colonies, European man quickly spread across the continent, pushing local populations of animals and humans into poorer habitats, or to extinction. In New Brunswick, walruses were wiped out as early as 1750; wolverines were gone by 1800; the eastern timber wolf by 1860, and woodland caribou by the 1920s; the last confirmed eastern panther was shot in the 1930s.

Man extirpated these animals by overhunting and poisoning them and by removing the forests that they required for shelter and food. On a local level, many other species have also been decimated, and such was the situation when Fundy National Park was established in 1948. In addition to the animals listed above, fisher, marten and peregrine falcons had disappeared, and Atlantic salmon were gone from the rivers. In order to return the park to a condition more closely resembling pre-European times, a number of these animals have been reintroduced.

Obviously, the wholesale stocking of all of the original kinds of animals to an area as small as the park could never succeed. Woodland caribou would not find enough food in the park and surrounding clearcuts, and the reintroduction of eastern wolves and panthers is impossible because of their unavailability, not to mention the problems of local resistance to such a scheme. At any rate, coyotes have introduced themselves to Fundy, and seem to be filling a place in the food chain left vacant by the extinction of the eastern timber wolf. Other smaller animals have needed help to return.

Atlantic Salmon

For almost a century, a dam at the mouth of the Point Wolfe River barred Atlantic salmon from spawning. In 1982, a four-year restoration program was launched by Parks Canada and the Department of Fisheries and Oceans. Each year, 42 000 fingerlings reared from the eggs of local salmon were carried to selected pools along the river by helicopter.

After growing for two years in the river, young salmon run to sea as silvery smolt, swimming downriver with the spring freshet. After a year or more at sea, a salmon has grown to maturity, and heads back to its home river. To allow returning grilse — salmon that have spent only one year at sea — and adult salmon to ascend the Point Wolfe River, a passage was cut in the Point Wolfe dam in 1984. The river was then closed to angling so that a healthy salmon population could become established. This is a rare opportunity indeed, considering the dwindling stocks of these fish throughout the North Atlantic. Bay of Fundy salmon may be quite different from others. Research seems to indicate that they spend their entire

Peregrine falcon

lives within Canadian territorial waters, perhaps never leaving the Bay of Fundy, a situation that offers them immunity from fishing on the high seas.

In time, and with protection, about 1500 salmon should fight their way upstream through the rapids and pools of the Point Wolfe River each year, and Fundy will become more complete for it. There are few other places that can help to preserve these magnificent fish, and right now salmon need all of the protection that they can get.

Peregrine Falcons

In the autumn of 1948, the last peregrine falcons to nest along the cliffs of Albert County left, never to return. The birds of kings, peregrine falcons are swift-flying, pointed-winged missiles which plummet at other birds as they fly. Striking their prey in midair in an explosion of feathers and talons, they kill instantly. Peregrines are extraordinary and beautiful predators.

At the top of a food pyramid, they feed on songbirds and shorebirds which eat insects and other invertebrates. Shortly after World War II, great strides were made in the chemical protection of crops, and farmers and foresters were quick to put these new products to use. One of the chemical "wonders" that found favour throughout North America at this time was Dichlorodiphenyltrichloroethane, or DDT. As insects fed on sprayed plants, the poisons built up in their bodies.

With each meal of poisoned insects, a warbler or other songbird could

Marten

accumulate a dose of poison many times more concentrated than that sprayed on the plants. In turn, peregrines ate the songbirds and were contaminated, and their eggs carried a fatal dose. Like the ospreys and eagles that shared their plight, the falcons' bodies were not able to cope with the poison. The results were reproductive failure and, finally, the abandonment of traditional nesting sites. By the late 1960s peregrine falcons were close to extinction in eastern North America.

In 1982, Fundy National Park and the Canadian Wildlife Service began a four-year co-operative program to re-establish these birds in the upper Bay of Fundy. Two former nesting sites were selected for the releases — one at Cap d'Or in Nova Scotia, and one in Fundy National Park, high on a cliff overlooking Point Wolfe cove. Five-week-old peregrine chicks raised at a facility in Alberta were delivered to the park and placed in a special cliffside nest box. The birds were fed for ten days with as little exposure to humans as possible; then the screen on the front of the box was opened and the birds were free to come and go as they liked. Food was left regularly at the box for another eight weeks while the birds taught themselves to fly and to catch live prey.

First flights were a tense occasion for both the birds and their guardians, but the peregrines learned fast, and were soon chasing anything that moved, from swallows and sparrows to ravens and great blue herons. By the end of the summer, the birds were fully independent and migrated south following their prey. It is hoped by everyone involved in the release, and by anyone who has watched these magnificent fliers, that they will return to nest. Perhaps the Bay of Fundy will once again become their most important breeding area in the Maritimes.

Marten

Larger than a weasel but smaller than a house cat, the marten is a golden brown member of the weasel family. Marten spend much of their time in trees and, like lumbermen, they prefer mature spruce forests. As the tall trees were felled and turned into ships and houses during the 1800s, the remaining scrubby forests provided only poor habitat. Those marten that survived in the dwindling bush were trapped for their skins. Sable coats were popular and expensive, and with a price on its head no animal can survive for long. Soon they were gone from most of southern New Brunswick.

During the winter of 1983–84, the trapping of marten continued in the north of the province. Six particular animals fell for the bait. Four males and two females were live-trapped by a Canadian Wildlife Service biologist and became the first marten involved in a two-year reintroduction program in Fundy National Park. They were held for two to three months in large cages in a suitable forest grove to let them get used to their new surroundings. Then, each fitted with a collar bearing a tiny radio transmitter, they were released.

Quick and quiet, they move with feline grace and feed at night on voles, squirrels, birds, insects and berries. Large owls, coyotes and fishers are their only predators.

Man has wrought many changes on this continent in the last few centuries, perhaps the greatest of which is the reduction of wilderness. Very soon only such places as national parks will remain unexploited, and even there the pressures of use are mounting yearly. National parks are refuges for wildlife, especially for those plants and animals with specialized needs for food, habitat and privacy. Moose and bison, for example, cannot adapt to man's encroachment in the same way that raccoons and skunks can.

Constantly used as a study area, Fundy has been searched for rare plants and animals, examined for budworm-resistant trees, and monitored for insecticide spray drift. Mammals are counted on a regular basis, parasites and diseases are studied, forest changes are measured, and mountains of information build up. We will probably never know all that we want to know about how wild plants and animals function and interact, but studies in protected areas give us some understanding of their relationships. National parks are becoming the most researched portions of land in the country, and it is all happening quietly in places like the forests and rivers of Fundy.

RIVERSONG

D eeply dissecting the upland plateau, the park's rivers, narrow and shallow, flow swiftly like mountain streams. Over a distance of about 20 km they descend 330 m to sea level. They accomplish this through long series of waterfalls and rapids interspersed with deep pools and fast-flowing bouldery shallows. Fundy's rivers are certainly not suitable for any form of boating, and were barely fit for driving logs. Gorges, right-angle bends, flat intervals and confluences add to the complexity of the rivers as they twist and turn, eroding their courses through bedrock, following faults, and carving deeply into softer rock. Where stymied by hard rock ledges, they are forced into waterfalls and flumes. This landscape of water and rock is the most diverse and exciting scenery in the park.

FROM FRESHET TO FREEZE-UP

The park's drainage system consists of two main rivers — the Point Wolfe and the Upper Salmon and their tributaries, and three smaller rivers — Goose River, Mile Brook and Dickson Brook. Frozen during the winter, these rivers come to life with the spring freshet as meltwater swells them over their banks. Melting snow cannot soak into the still-frozen soil, and is forced to trickle downhill in runnels and collect in valley bottoms. As millions of tonnes of snow are liquefied by the spring sun, the rivers quicken, then rush, then roar down to the sea. Water levels rise as much as 2 m above normal, and chunks of ice carried by the frigid torrents smash against the banks, dislodging rocks, crushing plants and ripping bark off streamside trees. In the valley bottoms, the only plants that survive are those that can repair such damage quickly, or those that grow on the protected downstream side of large rocks. Many river valley plants die down to deep underground roots or rhizomes and thus escape the tumult of the spring thaw. Trout and young salmon (fingerlings, parr and smolt) seek

Point Wolfe dam during freshet

sheltered places and hover there in the debris-filled waters to avoid being swept downstream. Waterfalls and rapids swell and become tea-coloured cascades. Rivers thunder off the uplands, dropping loads of gravel and sand as they slow down on the flatter lowlands and sheet out over valley bottoms.

Icy water is discharged into the bay from the mouths of rivers, streaking the silty bay with colour. Logs, ice cakes and other winter wreckage wash out to sea and bob for days or weeks until waterlogged, or marooned ashore, tens of kilometres from their origin. The freshet usually lasts for a few weeks in April. Then the soil warms and soaks up the last of the thawing snow and ice, and the rivers slow and begin to clear as sediment settles to the bottom. Life returns to normal for the fish and water insects. Spring is upon them again.

Summer on the rivers is a time of warmth. During the day, the sun heats the rocks and the water that streams over them. Reduced water levels make walking along the riverbanks an exercise in rock-hopping and shallow wading. Stained by percolation through forest soil, river water is a light brown colour. Sunlight streams through the riffles, marking the riverbeds with shifting patterns of gold laciness. Backwaters turn green as feathery algae sprout in their warmth, while deep pools lie quiet and black, inviting swimmers to explore with diving masks and snorkels. Often, heavy rains will raise water levels dramatically, up to a metre within forty-eight hours. As water sheets off the uplands and pours down the narrow valleys, it can create hazardous fording conditions, swelling unimpressive trickles into racing flumes.

As river waters cool and the last autumn leaves pirouette through the rapids, life in the rivers slows down. Many riverside animals and river-bottom insects go into a sort of hibernation to avoid the rigours of winter. Fish seek the largest pools so that they will be below the level of ice.

Only with the coming of winter does the water go quiet. In the deep cold the rivers resemble flat white roads snaking through the valleys, twisting towards the sea. Occasionally a wisp of vapour can be seen rising from a still dripping waterfall, the face of the falls a mass of translucent ice pillars shrouded in the eerie fog. A trickling of frigid water is often the only sound, save for the occasional crack of frozen trees and the creak of stepped-on snow.

A World Apart

A river valley is a closed-in world. The only horizons are the tops of the nearest hills, and the sun sets behind them hours early plunging the valley into cool blue shade. Outside sound is muffled by the constant murmur of flowing water, and movement is made difficult by boulders, water and slippery algae. Yet nowhere else in the park does one get the same feeling of wildness, vigour and variety.

An almost subliminal aspect of a hike down one of the rivers is its noise. There is a constant background of sound from the rivers and streams. The thunder of a waterfall in full flow gives way downstream to the splash of water in rapids, and farther still to the gurgle of a stream flowing smoothly over and around rocks. River water is always talking. Often one does not notice it until moving away from the river on a trail, when ears ring with the quiet.

There is a special smell too, the smell of water drying on rocks, of riverside pools bubbling with algae, of trees, fresh ferns and grasses, of moist stream banks, and the faint, sweet scent of wild orchids.

RIVERWATER AND TIME, MASTER CARVERS OF STONE

For more than one-and-a-half million years, these rivers have drained the highlands. Scratching away at the hard rock with water-borne sand grains, they have sculpted the once-flat plateau into a series of rolling uplands. Steep rock walls, narrow gorges and deeply worn plunge pools below waterfalls testify to the power of water over rock. In the gorge below the covered bridge on the Fortyfive River is a pothole worn 6 m deep and 5 m wide into the solid rock. On the East Branch River is another, below the double-tiered Upper Slewgundy Falls. Along the course of the Broad River, between Big Dam and the Fortyfive River, numerous smooth-sided pools have been scoured. Two deep potholes have been worn by the triple-tiered Bennett Brook Falls. Over the ages this falls has eroded a rock

BRIAN TOWNSEND

Dickson Falls

amphitheatre which encloses a dark pool at its base. Steep gravelly river-banks sometimes succumb to erosion and collapse as narrow debris chutes or avalanches, nearly blocking the rivers below.

A glance at the park map (pp. 98–99) shows twenty-four waterfalls. These are the most impressive or most easily reached falls in the park, nearly all over 5 m in height. Few of the park's falls have names, and there are many more than appear on the map. The tallest is Third Vault Falls, at 17 m. A narrow cascade, it splits in two as it pours down the rock face into

Pitcher plant

Blue violet

Purple-fringed orchid

Blue-flag iris

a cold pool. It is particularly beautiful during the winter when blue ice curtains and pillars cling to the rock, enshrouded in a crystalline mist. A second, equally impressive falls can be seen just upstream. A few kilometres to the north is Laverty Falls, a wide curtain of water that is at its best after a heavy rain.

The most accessible waterfall in the park is a small one at Herring Cove, just a couple of minutes' walk south of the parking lot on the Coastal Trail. Pouring over slanted sandstones into a ravine that it has gouged out, the brook flows out onto Herring Cove beach at the midpoint of the Cove Trail loop. Dickson Falls is also just a few minutes' walk from its parking lot, and is part of the most popular short trail in the park.

The park's most scenic hiking is along three stretches of river: the lower half of Bennett Brook, the Broad River from Laverty Brook to the Fortyfive River and the Point Wolfe River from where Bennett Brook joins it to just above its confluence with the East Branch. Strenuous hiking over rugged terrain will get you into these sites, and the exertion is worth it. In some places the banks are so narrow and sheer that it is necessary to climb around or wade a section of river. No trails follow the banks, so the hike becomes a private exploration.

LIFE AT THE WATER'S EDGE

Along the rocky valley sides sprout some of the less common trees and shrubs of the park — ash, eastern white cedar, striped maple, mountain maple, yew and, on dry sites, white pine. Thickets of speckled alder crowd the edges of floodplains, places where other shrubs or trees would be torn loose by ice in spring. Clinging to calcium-rich cliffs that border sections of the rivers are roseroot, wild purple clematis, creeping juniper, fir clubmoss, poison ivy and fragrant cliff-fern, well out of the reach of both high water and people.

Spray from waterfalls and the constant seep of cliffside springs promotes the growth of moisture-loving plants. Rock walls around plunge pools are often covered with a fuzzy mantle of mosses, liverworts and ferns. Cool, shaded conditions favour these plants and exclude most common forest species. Here and there a tree does manage to grow, but only as a crack-hugging bonsai.

Better growing conditions are found on the flood plains. There, thick layers of soil have been deposited by countless spring floods. Valley-bottom trees often grow larger than those in thin forest soils, and beneath them a community of deep-rooting plants has developed — wood anemone, ostrich fern, oak fern, cow parsnip, red and white baneberry, starry Solomon's-seal and many other spring flowers and ferns.

Smoothed by uncountable spring thaws, polished, colourful river rocks jut from the banks or lie half submerged in water. Around their bases and sheltered beneath them live myriad small insects. Favourite food of trout and young salmon, stoneflies, mayflies and caddisflies search for food and try to avoid being eaten by fish and each other. The fisherman's artificial flies of feathers, wool and silk mimic these common river insects.

The variety of adaptations that insects make to different river environments is extraordinary. Caddisflies alone present endless variations in the protective cases they build. Fast water forms build tubular cases of sand and fine pebbles, or anchor themselves to boulders inside tiny stone igloos. Others live in cracks between rocks and catch food with beautifully woven conical silk nets, resembling those used by butterfly collectors. In quieter streams and pools, other species of caddisflies build cylindrical "log cabins," or they fit pieces of stick and bark together to disguise themselves as twigs. In spite of this instinctive guile, many end up as fish food.

Along the downstream side of rocks that poke out of rapids are the wormlike larvae and hard black pupae of blackflies. The adult flies are able to make even the least interested visitor take notice, but the juvenile forms usually escape unseen. They require the oxygen-rich water of rapids to bring them food, which they snare in comblike fans as the water rushes

Small pools along riversides are used by toads and frogs as mating ponds and nurseries. Often these puddles are black with writhing tadpoles that graze on the algae that coat the stones. Between pools grow thick tufts of sedges and grasses, and in these, where the soil has not been removed by water and ice, live wild orchids. From mid-June to July, leafy white orchids and purple fringed orchids bloom; both are tall plants with fragrant, showy flower spikes. Mixed with them are yellow buttercups, joe-pye weed, blue flag iris, meadow rue, and various blue and white asters and yellow goldenrods.

In late July, Atlantic salmon begin to move up the rivers to spawn. Although once blocked by dams, park rivers are now for the most part free-flowing. Salmon lie in the deepest pools, staying cool and preparing for the mating and egg laying that will take place in November. Sometimes as many as sixty fish will rest in a large pool, lying close to the bottom, stacked four or five deep, moving only when annoyed or startled. Red, yellow, orange and brown leaves swirl downstream in a constant parade around the waiting salmon. As the eggs and sperm ripen within their bodies, the salmon leave the pools and begin to search for suitable gravel-bottomed shallows to dig their redds. After the eggs are laid, fertilized and covered with gravel, the salmon drift downstream to the sea. Some die from exhaustion and wounds. But as many as 20 per cent survive the stress of spawning and live to feed, recover, and prepare for their next mating run. Some have returned as many as six times.

High waterfalls on the upper reaches of both the Point Wolfe–East Branch and Upper Salmon–Broad River systems block even the muscular Atlantic salmon as they return from the sea. However, pencil-sized eels are able to surmount them. These elvers, dark above and silvery below, enter the rivers after hatching and growing for about a year at sea. When they reach waterfalls, they lunge upward from rock to rock in the moisture beneath the cascading water. Sometimes they leave the water completely and squirm through moss and rock rubble, resting and pushing ahead, falling backward and trying again until they reach the top. Fighting their

Atlantic salmon

way in a struggle that puts salmon to shame, they move into the very headwaters of rivers and streams, and there live out most of their adult lives. Graceful and fast, the Atlantic eel can startle but not harm a swimmer. The only defences that these bottom-dwelling fish have are speed and a thick slippery skin. They feed on small fish, insects and almost anything else they can scavenge. Eels live inland for nine or ten years before migrating downriver to the bay, then to the Sargasso Sea, south of Bermuda, where, thousands of kilometres from home, they lay their eggs — and die.

Brook, or speckled, trout are most often seen in shaded streams and in lakes. They lie in the deep pools below waterfalls, in the dark riffles behind boulders, and in the streamside tangles of overarching alders. Small schools of these fish mark time in the flowing water until a movement alerts them to an insect drifting downstream. In a flash, the insect is engulfed by a hungry trout, and the fish returns to its place in the school. From above, trout are so well camouflaged that they are hard to see, but their gold, red, white and green colouration makes them a favourite with those who watch fish underwater.

Brook trout, salmon and eels are not just the most common fish that occur naturally in Fundy's rivers and lakes, but the *only* fish. Rivers, streams and lakes were rendered barren by the last ice age. When it ended, in order for fish to recolonize the rivers of the upper bay, they had to move through the bay's salt water and find suitable habitat. Fundy's fast-flowing cold streams have not proved attractive to the pickerel, bass, catfish, dace, chub, shiners and suckers that are found in rivers just down the coast. Mummichogs and sticklebacks live in the river estuaries, but never venture farther upstream.

Dragonfly

Tiger swallowtails at a mineral lick

THE WETLANDS

At Fundy, the river valleys are pathways to the heart of the park. If you follow a river up from the sea, you will eventually find the lake, bog or spring that is its source. Wet places such as these are few and small in the park because of the fast drainage that the river valleys provide.

Largest of the park's ten small lakes and five ponds are Wolfe and

Bennett lakes. In the years before the park was established, both were dammed to raise their water levels, and the dams are maintained to this day. Three islets dot Bennett Lake, providing a destination for boaters and swimmers. Wolfe Lake has one small island. Neither lake is much deeper than 11 m; their average depth is about 3 m. Water in park lakes and ponds often looks deeper than it actually is due to the dark golden stain that water picks up as it percolates through decomposing vegetation in the soil.

During the two decades following the park's establishment, both brook trout and a small number of western rainbow trout were stocked in lakes and ponds. Each year, thousands of hatchery fish were dumped into the lakes, and quickly consumed much of the natural food. Then, because they were not as wary as wild fish, they were yanked out in the first few weeks of fishing season. What wild trout survived in the lakes were stunted for lack of food. This unnatural stocking was halted in 1981 to give the native fish a chance to grow.

Deepest of the park's water bodies is a lake so small that it bears the name MacLaren Pond. Originally known as Edgett's Lake, it was renamed to honour the Lieutenant Governor of New Brunswick at the time that the park was established. Known to geologists as a kettle lake, it formed at the end of the last ice age. As the continental glaciers melted, they shed their burden of rock and gravel in torrents of icy water. Large fragments broke from the melting ice sheet and were quickly buried by the slurry of water and rock. The ice chunks, insulated by this stony blanket, took decades to melt. As the ice gradually turned to water, the covering layers of debris caved in, forming an almost circular, deep, steep-sided pond. Since its formation, the pond has been filling in with mud and organic sediments. Although it has been called a bottomless lake, it is now only about 13 m deep.

Bogs are also relics of the ice age. Moving ice scraped depressions in the rock. These became lakes and ponds when the ice melted and the drainage channels were blocked by dams of rock and gravel. Moss spores, borne north on the wind, grew in the cool, moist depressions. Year by year, peaty layers of sphagnum moss accumulated, preserved with only a small amount of decomposition by the acidic, oxygen-poor bog water. Now, after 10 000 years of growth, the skin of living moss that builds the bog floats atop sodden peaty deposits many metres thick. Because there is little decomposition, bogs preserve a relatively complete record of thousands of years of their own growth and development. They also record changes in the forest around them. Pollen grains, seeds, leaves, charcoal from fires and even the remains of animals may rest hidden beneath the moss.

Largest of the bogs in the park is Caribou Plain, named for the wood-land caribou that once wintered in the area. It is now crossed by a boardwalk trail. In the middle of the bog, dwarf black spruce and larch trees grow, stunted by the wet peaty soil. Some of these trees have lived here for more than a century without growing any taller than a child. Most have been rendered infertile by lack of nutrients, and will never set seed. Many of the spruce have also been parasitized by hundreds of centimetre-long dwarf mistletoe plants.

Other bog plants have found ways to supplement their meagre diets by catching and consuming animals. Carnivorous plants are usually after only one thing — nitrogen. Although there is plenty of nitrogen in the air, most plants cannot extract it, and rely on algae and bacteria that can. But these organisms cannot live in bog soils, and so bog plants either make do without nitrogen or take it from another rich source — the protein in animal bodies. Pitcher plants trap insects in hollow leaves. Nectar glands draw flies to the plants, and as they walk around the leaves, they slip and eventually drown in the water-filled "pitchers." There they are digested by bacteria and by enzymes secreted by these plant "stomachs." The tiny, glistening red leaves of sundews, another type of carnivorous plant, attract insects. Glue secreted by leaf-hairs captures flies and ants. When triggered by a struggling insect, the leaf slowly wraps around its prey and digests it.

Boggy ponds and sluggish streams harbour bladderworts, their long trailing stems covered with hair-like leaves and globular traps. Small water-animals that brush against triggers on these traps activate a lightning-fast mechanism. A lid pops open, water and animal are sucked inside, and then the lid slams shut. All this happens in the blink of an eye with traps the size of sesame seeds.

Yellow pond lilies grow well in shallow bog ponds and lakes, trailing thick underwater stems along the bottom as they spread. These soft rhizomes, which grow to the size of a man's arm, are a favourite food of moose and beaver. Moose visit the lakes in early morning to wade and dive for these succulent sweets. Half-eaten stems often wash up on shore where they are slowly consumed by pond snails. An unusual mottled northern frog — the mink frog — inhabits the mossy edges of these ponds, feeding on insects that hatch from the water.

Lakes and bogs brimming with brown water lie placid under the warm sun. In the rocky gorges, springs seep through a deep plush of dark green moss, dripping wet crystals that flash in the sunlight. Runnels gurgle quietly through shady forest groves as water-striders skate across their surfaces. Streams, quick with trout, race between boulders and roots and under ferny overhangs. Rivers twist and turn through deep valleys, then plunge over the lips of falls and crash into black pools below. Rivers grown wide and shallow finish their migration to the sea by riffling over gravel and boulders, then mixing with the salt and silt of the bay. Fundy's wild rivers and streams are its most beautiful and changeable features.

WHEN THE TALL TREES FELL

O n a warm day in Fundy National Park nothing is more relaxing than to sit near the edge of a secluded cliff and take in the fresh air, the sun and the scenery. Far below, sparkles drift across the water's surface into the hazy blue distance. The throb of a fishing boat engine intrudes, but soon fades away as the boat rounds a headland. Waves slosh rhythmically against beach cobbles, and soon, sun-warmed eyelids are lulled shut. The present disappears, but in the mind's eye the past becomes visible.

PASSAGES

. . . a child's laugh and the hollow slap of wavelets against a boat — along the shore comes a small flotilla of birch-bark canoes. Hugging the coast and carefully watching for rocks, three Micmac families move up the shoreline route called Goolwagakwek to hunt at the marshes known as Esedebit. Passing quickly by the uninviting rocky coast, the Indians do not stop to rest, but push on. This rough land offers them nothing that cannot be found more easily elsewhere. Soon they are out of sight.

1605: Creaking ropes and the squeal of wood rubbing against wood — Samuel de Champlain's ungainly sailing ship ploughs slowly before a weak breeze, all sails set. It shows the signs of a rough ocean crossing to this "Baie Française." One small figure on deck is taking measurements from a hand-held instrument; another records his readings. Perhaps Vikings and others had paid earlier visits, but these men are exploring the bay anew. Basque, Breton and Portuguese fishermen visited the bay for generations before its official "discovery," but, like the Indians, they left few marks of their passage. These men, however, will leave a record. Their map will be crude, but any map tames the unknown and invites others to continue the exploration.

1699: A roughly copied map flutters in his hands as the helmsman of a bobbing shallop tries to match vague ink lines to the reality of the rock-bound coast. Pierre Thibaudeau and his three sons had bid adieu to Port Royal (in 1710 this name was changed to Annapolis Royal N.S.), the first attempt at permanent settlement in New France, and are heading for a new home farther up the bay. Founded by Pierre Du Gua, Sieur de Monts and his lieutenant, Samuel de Champlain, in 1605, Port Royal had grown fast, and by the 1690s, families like Thibaudeau's were spreading to sites all around the bay. Marshlands were favoured since they could be dyked, drained of salt water, and then farmed — a much easier chore than taming the thin rocky soils held by the forest. Thibaudeau is sailing for a marsh that his sons had admired while fur trading in the upper bay — a place that the Indians called Esedebit, known to the Acadians as Chipoudie (Shepody). Here they will dyke marshland, build a gristmill and sawmill and start a village. The Micmac and Malecite Indians are friendly, the marshes extensive, and trading should be good since the village of Beaubassin is just across the bay, and another, called Petitcodiac, is being built upriver. At last they will be far from the eternal squabbles between England and France over ownership of the New World.

Unfortunately it is not to be — within the lifetime of Pierre's sons, the peaceful existence of the Acadian communities will be shattered.

1704: Trading can be a risky business, especially when it is done with the enemy. This is the eighth year that the New England trader has sailed north in his small ship into French territory to do business with the Acadians. Frowned upon by the British governor in Boston, and officially banned by the French authorities at Quebec and Port Royal, the trade is essential to the colonists of both countries. Dodging warships and bartering manufactured goods, ironware, spices, salt and rum for such items as grain, livestock, fish, feathers and furs, a number of traders ply these waters. So do privateers — official pirates commissioned by the British government to harass the Acadians in retaliation for French-led Indian raids against the New England colonies. The privateers sail under letters of marque, and raid towns and settlements all along the coast, breaching dykes, killing livestock, sacking and burning as they go.

This year the trader's timing is bad. Privateers out of Boston have struck his last three stops, razing half the village of Beaubassin, and there is little left to trade. This will not to be a good year for him and will be worse for the Acadians. Without animals, crops or implements, they will have to rebuild.

1755: The worst has happened. A decade after the fall of the Fortress of Louisbourg, an order has come through for the deportation of all Acadians who refuse to pledge allegiance to the British Crown. Since 1713, when Acadia fell to the British by the Treaty of Utrecht, attempts have been made to secure the Acadians' loyalty. After a hundred years in this new land they, like the New England colonists, feel themselves a nation apart. They will keep the peace, but they will not pledge to bear arms against the French or the Indians.

For the sake of security in this war-torn century, the British governors of the colonies of Massachusetts and Nova Scotia (the latter included New Brunswick until 1784, and was the English name for what had been Acadie) decide to end this problem forever. Marshalled by British and New England troops, some sympathetic and some vindictive, the nation of Acadia is broken apart. Boats move down the bay carrying grief-stricken Acadians to exile in the English-speaking southern colonies. Soon most of the Acadians will be gone from ''Acadie'' — the villages of Memramcook, Petitcodiac and Chipoudie will be no more. These boatloads of refugees straggling past Fundy's cliffs mark the end of an era and the beginning of a legend.

1760s: For a while the bay is quiet, save for the occasional small boat. Immigrants arrive at Halifax from Europe and the British-American colonies, where trouble is brewing. Much good dyked farmland is available through land grant in the upper bay, and soon families arrive overland and by boat to resettle the ghost villages. A group of Germans from New England (Pennsylvania Deutsch, or ''Dutch'') take land along the Petitcodiac River and soon establish three townsites. Irish, English and Scottish immigrants arrive too, all looking for land to call their own and a new start in the new country. The wars that have occupied England for half a century have also drained her coffers, and a tax called the Stamp Act is passed in the American Colonies to raise money. Relationships between New England and the British colonies to the north quickly sour.

In New England, a rebel government calling itself the Continental Congress sets itself up in 1775 in opposition to British rule. Attacks are made against British garrisons at Montreal and Quebec, and the revolutionaries seek sympathizers among New Englanders recently settled around the Bay of Fundy. British ships of war patrol the bay to prevent sabotage and to deter American privateers. All strangers are suspect, and loyalist refugees flood northward into Nova Scotia.

A rebel general, George Washington, sends envoys north to try to arouse the Indians to guerilla war, but the Indians trust the American colonists even less than they do the British. Jonathan Eddy, rebel sympathizer from the town of Chignecto, gathers a force of more than one hundred other traitors and attacks Fort Cumberland (the English name for Fort Beausejour near today's Amherst, N.S.). Just in time, His Majesty's ship *Vulture* sails up the bay and arrives at the poorly defended fort, quickly routing the rebels. Eddy and a band of his men flee along an old military route to sanctuary in Saint John. Less than twenty-five years after trying to force the Acadians to take an oath of allegiance, the Nova Scotia government has to impose the same oath on its English-speaking subjects.

(Louis XVI of France had strongly backed the American rebel cause; it

Kinnie farm, Butland settlement, ca. 1905

is a curious twist that France was an instrument in gaining independence for the English colonies whose annihilation she had worked so hard to attain a few years earlier. Ironic too that this king lost his head when his own subjects followed the American example of republicanism.)

Loyalist refugees from the American colonies continue to pour into Halifax. From there they disperse to the rest of the colony. In Nova Scotia and Canada, they are able to express their royalist opinions without being robbed, tarred and feathered, or hanged. These experienced settlers, many of them businessmen and politicians, receive land grants and try to rebuild in the wilds of Nova Scotia the society that they have recently left. Many of them quickly prosper. Their wishes to be free from the control of Halifax and to follow personal political aspirations are accommodated by the partition of Nova Scotia into two provinces: New Brunswick is established by an Order in Council in 1784. Strange fate, that the colonies first settled by British subjects in North America were lost, while those first settled by the French became part of the Commonwealth.

1800: Far down the bay a schooner is running before the wind. Saint John has grown fast and hundreds of ships have crossed the Atlantic carrying timber to Britain. Rather than return empty, they offer inexpensive passage to Canada, attracting Scottish, Irish and English emigrants. From the docks at Saint John, families set out to claim land grants all around the new colony of New Brunswick. Many take the Shepody or ''Immigrants'' Road, one of the oldest roads in the colony, linking Saint John to the settlements along Shepody Bay. Villages like Donegal, Londonderry and New Ireland and nameless clusters of farmsteads dot the wilderness, strung like beads along

Fieldstone foundation marks old homesite

the thin dirt track. Wolves and caribou still roam the forests, and life for most of the backwoods settlers is hard and short.

Sinklers (Sinclairs), Gallaghers, Alcorns, McKinleys and others with names now forgotten arrive as tradesmen, shopkeepers and tinkers. Soon they become hardscrabble settlers along the Shepódy and other roads, trying to eke a living from the rocky soil during brief growing seasons, knowing that somewhere conditions have to be better.

BAYSHORE BEGINNINGS

Conditions were perfect for a lumber mill at the mouth of the Point Wolf River. (The spelling was officially changed to Wolfe in 1956.) John Ward, a Loyalist late of New York, who became a rich businessman-politician in Saint John, was quick to establish one. Unexploited wilderness for well-nigh ten thousand years, by 1826 the mill town of Point Wolf was founded and the forest was falling to build Saint John — and John Ward's fortune. In all, about forty schooners worked the bay, moving fresh-sawn timber from small mills like those at Point Wolf, Goose River, and others at the mouth of almost every river that emptied into the bay.

Settlement of the Alma area was started by squatters around 1825. The first real clearing of farmland was done by Otis Cannon who obtained a grant one kilometre down the coast from the present village at a place that came to be known as Cannon Town (where the swimming pool is today). Cannon soon built a small brook-powered sawmill and a tide-powered fishing weir. At the same time, a community grew around the mouth of the Salmon River (now the Upper Salmon River), with family names such as

Martin, Kinnie and Cleveland. By 1836, the first mill was built on the river, and the village of Salmon River (Alma) began to bustle.

Tracks, not roads, led from settlement to settlement, and farms began to grow along them. Up the now uninhabited Fortyfive Road was the settlement of Sinclair Hill, and another small community sprang up at Herring Cove.

On the Shepody Road, conditions were not as good for farming as along the coast. One surveyor described the land thus: "The land on the road is middling, but the rears is poor." Winter on the uplands in cramped and drafty cabins, heated only by poorly constructed fireplaces, must have been a six-month misery of lonely, white isolation.

Many of the settlers were recent arrivals from towns and cities in Britain and not used to the deprivation. Families that had settled along the Shepody Road soon started to abandon their farms. After 1834, a steady trickle of people shifted from the cold highlands to the more forgiving coast, swelling the communities of Salmon River and Herring Cove.

The story of one of these families is typical of the times: James McKinley and Rose Eliza Kyle were fellow passengers on the trip across the Atlantic from the north of Ireland. They landed at Saint John, and were married in 1833. James had been a silk merchant in Ireland and hoped to pursue his trade in British North America. Silk was not, however, a commodity that many of the struggling settlers in New Brunswick needed or could afford. "Pedlar" McKinley would have to look for another profession. Shortly, he and Eliza set off by coach down the Immigrant Road to farm a small grant of land they were able to obtain. Where they were dropped off must have looked grim, but they set about clearing some land close to the road, erecting a small house and planting a garden. Inexperienced as farmers and faced with poor soils and hard winters, the couple did not prosper as they had hoped, though a child was born to them there.

According to the story passed on by their descendants, within a couple of years of settling in the uplands, James, Eliza and their child weathered a particularly hard winter. That spring James set off on foot through deep snow to try to obtain supplies along the coast. As he got closer to the bay, he noticed that much of the snow had melted, and that the mayflowers were in bloom.

On his return he must have discussed his discovery with Eliza, and as soon as the weather warmed they loaded up their possessions and set off for the coast. They followed the trail that is now the Fortyfive Road, with James leading their mule laden with belongings, and Eliza carrying their baby. After passing through the village of Salmon River (Alma), they crossed the river and walked up into what is now the park. There they followed the cart track towards Point Wolf, past Cannon Town, along the valley of Dickson

Brook, and up a steep hill to the brook along which they wished to settle. As it was getting dark, they made camp for the evening. That night it rained hard, and the small family spent the night huddled together beneath an umbrella in the shelter of a large maple tree. Their prospects soon brightened, however, and by that July of 1835 they had settled on a 100-acre lot. Within two years, a wide clearing had been cut and two buildings were erected.

The most-prized land grants were those along the coast where rivers or streams entered the bay, and these were taken first. Most transportation was by boat or ship, and running water was one of the few sources of power available; human and animal were the other two. The later the date of arrival of the settler, the farther inland was his plot, the poorer the site, and the more difficult the access. The best farmland in the park was owned by members of the Matthews family. John Matthews was one of the first settlers to arrive, and he obtained a grant of land at Herring Cove where a small brook enters the bay. The soil there was deeper and richer than on the surrounding land. The farm developed quickly, and soon the farmhouse was surrounded by outbuildings and sheds for livestock. A wharf was built for mooring the boats necessary for transportation, and the farm produced good crops of potatoes and grain. John Matthews's son Thomas was granted a lot to the west of his father's in another excellent location, known today as Matthews Head.

A flood of immigrants arrived from Ireland in the 1840s, driven from their homeland by politics and by a microscopic fungus that caused their main staple, potatoes, to rot in the fields and in storage. Cholera-ridden "coffin ships," some with survival records worse than those of the slavers, carried Irish settlers away from the Potato Famine and to British North America. After a period of quarantine, they made the Immigrant Road busy once again. Settlers pushed into the interior — to the uncut forest — initiating a period of rapid land clearing, forest levelling and community growth. A trail was soon open from the Salmon River–Point Wolf Road to the highlands. The lower stretch was settled and given the name of Hastings; its upper part became the Laverty Road. A spur trail ran to the home of Benjamin Bennett at the lake that now bears his name. This road would become the highway which now crosses the park. One of Bennett's children, W. A. C. Bennett, later moved west and became premier of British Columbia from 1952 to 1972.

After this period of growth and development throughout southern New Brunswick, the County of Albert was created in 1845, named after Albert, Prince consort to Queen Victoria. Ten years later the Parish of Alma was declared, containing most of the land that lies today within the park. The parish was named after the Battle of Alma, a British victory in the Crimean War the previous year. The village of Salmon River changed its name to Alma in 1875. In 1867, the colony of New Brunswick joined in a confederation with Upper and Lower Canada and Nova Scotia to protect itself from Fenian raiders (Irish-Americans intent on worrying British troops in an attempt to gain independence for Ireland) and the imperialist ambitions of the newly reunited American States to the south.

FISH AND WOODCHIPS

All the while, lumber mills continued to process the forest into boards. Mill trash — sawdust, edges, slabs and other debris — was dumped by most sawmills without burning. By the 1850s, vast amounts of waste fouled river mouths, ruining feeding and spawning grounds in the bay, and clogging fishermen's nets and weirs. No fishways were provided to help salmon, smelt, gaspereau and striped bass move up rivers and over mill dams to their spawning beds. A description of an 1852 visit to the area by M. H. Perley, the provincial fisheries officer, indicated the gravity of the problem:

> Point Wolf River is a large stream, of similar character with that of the other rivers of this coast. Like those rivers also, a substantial and rather lofty mill-dam prevents all fish from ascending, although many salmon yet enter the large basin beneath the dam. The saw mills are on an extensive scale; they belong to Messrs. Vernon, of Saint John, who procure their supply of logs within twelve miles of the mills. Owing to the difficulty of floating down logs in 1849, from the want of water, the millmen were idle during part of the summer; from lack of other occupation, they were employed in constructing a weir on the flats within the bar. In this weir, nearly 500 salmon were caught during that season; of these, 21 breeding fish, heavy with spawn, were taken alive, and carefully conveyed in casks of water, to the river above the dam, into which they were turned without injury. This was a very judicious step towards preserving the salmon fishery of this fine river; but it is greatly to be regretted, that Messrs. Vernon have not already set up, and maintained a sufficient fishway. The supply of logs decreases annually, and after a time will cease altogether; but if the salmon are preserved, they will prove a source of wealth, long after the saw mills are worn out and useless.

Because the lumber industry was so important to the colony's economy, mill owners held tremendous political sway. Regardless of what legislation was implemented, the lumber barons paid no attention. Declining fish populations and clogged nets, traps, and weirs brought an end to the fishery of the upper Bay of Fundy.

During the winter, as many as sixty lumber teams worked in the woods, piling logs on the ice and banks of nearby streams. When rivers and streams were too far away, the men cut chutes down steep hillsides to the closest channel and stacked the logs in huge "brows" at the top. The

Point Wolf Mill, ca. 1910

freshet in the spring would flush logs from the river beds down to the mill. After these logs had been moved, the logs up in the brows would be released, to cascade down to the river beds. A series of dams held some of the freshet water back for just this moment. When all of the brows had been broken, the dams were opened one by one — the timing and order were crucial — and a great flush of water would move down the river valley, lifting the logs and sluicing them towards the mill pond. Logs that had lodged along the banks were worked back into the water by men with peaveys. Jams had to be pried loose carefully, for drowning in the icy water or death by crushing were two very real hazards of the job. During the drives, waterfalls, bends and gorges in the narrow river valleys earned names they bear to this day. The Keyhole, Matchfactory and Hell's Gates are relics of this era, as are Big Dam, Upper and Lower Slewgundy and Moosehorn Portage. When the logs reached the mill pond they were left there afloat, and the mill team took over. As logs were cut in the mill, others could be floated into position for an endless spurred chain to carry them up to the saws.

After a series of changes in ownership, the water-powered Point Wolf mill was modernized in 1884 and fitted out with boilers for steam power. This allowed the mill to run at peak capacity even when water levels were low. The mill was built atop the dam — spanning the river — and a rickety bridge crossed upstream from it. Fifty men worked in the mill day and night at the height of the season, sawing the logs and moving boards, lath and deal (planks) onto loading wharves that had been built in the

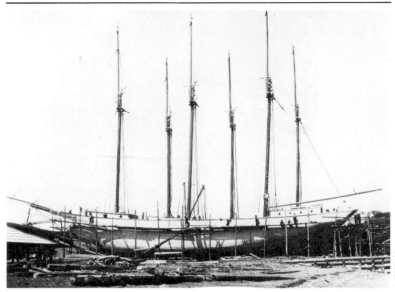

A. HASLAM

Twin schooners under construction, Alma Beach shipyard, 1918

gorge below the dam. From there lighters and small sailing ships could be loaded at high tide. Larger schooners could dock at an 80-m-long wharf built on the bar just downriver from the gorge. Lumber was hauled to it by scow and offloaded for storage on the dock until a schooner arrived. Three schooners were employed steadily for the Saint John market and two for the American market. Above the mill, the village of Point Wolf had expanded from the original company-owned shanties and fish shack. There were now homes, a boarding house for the men, a smithy and, of course, a company store. The company store was the source of most manufactured goods and also functioned as a post office, community centre and bank. Working men were paid each July through the store, where they had an open account. Their ''July pay'' often amounted to little or nothing once the balance between their account and their wages had been tallied. It was not uncommon for a workman to end up owing the millowner on payday.

Lumbering and shipbuilding were closely intertwined throughout the 1800s. Trees provided the raw material for ships, and ships provided the transport for lumber. Cleveland Brook runs through Alma, and at its mouth the town's first shipyard was established. From the 1850s to the 1890s, twenty schooners, brigs and barques were built there. Most towns and villages around the bay built ships, and Alma's shipyard was comparatively small. Nevertheless, shipbuilding was very important to the community. It was a focus for skilled craftsmen and an industry that forged pride in the community. It brought in tradesmen and sailors from outside, and formed a link between Alma and the rest of the world, bursting the confines of southern Albert County.

Few people held year-round jobs. Most men worked in the lumber camps in the winter, when logs could easily be hauled over roads of snow and ice and stacked in brows to await spring thaw. After the spring drive was over they would either farm their homesteads, or find work at a mill, on the wharves or perhaps on a schooner. Around Alma and Point Wolf the soils were neither deep nor fertile enough for farming to provide more than a subsistence living.

As early as 1873, a migration out of Albert County had begun. The lack of new horizons or economic opportunities in the country spurred youth to leave for cities in central Canada, the West or the United States. The movement away from farms left deserted fields and orchards, and was known locally as "the exodus." The last parts of Alma Parish to be settled were the first to be abandoned. Homesteads were sold to the lumber companies for whatever they would give, often less than a hundred dollars, and the population of the parish began to wither back towards the coastline.

Alma's shipyards fell quiet in 1889 during a world-wide merchant marine depression. This collapse, combined with the loss of the fishery and the ever-more-difficult task of obtaining trees for the mills, painted a bleak future for the bayshore settlements. The law of diminishing returns had caught up with the lumber industry.

In the 1890s, coal, gold and copper mining were tried, but only one mine near Point Wolf village ever produced much. Copper and some gold and silver were removed from milky quartz veins that ran through the hard rock. After nineteen years, the veins ran out.

At the turn of the century, the Alma and Point Wolf mills were bought by C. T. White, an entrepreneur who owned mills all around the bay. He modernized both mills, and things began to improve. Just before World War I, however, the business passed to his inexperienced son, Garfield.

The Whites brought shipbuilding back to Alma. The war created a vessel shortage that revived shipbuilding and reopened shipyards all along the eastern coast. Wharves and ways were constructed on the sand bar on the west side of the Salmon River's mouth, and from 1917 to 1919 four vessels were built. First constructed were the three-masted sisterships (schooners or terns) the *Vincent White* and the *Meredith White*. They sold quickly, prompting the building of two more ships in 1919, the barquentine *Whiteson* and the four-masted schooner *Bessie A. White*. Unfortunately, the shipbuilding renaissance was short-lived as markets soured for both lumber and wooden ships. Against all advice, Garfield White decided to stockpile lumber and hold onto ships that had not yet sold until better market conditions prevailed. He soon had 30 000 000 board feet of lumber in storage at Alma, while prices continued to plummet. In 1921, the *Whiteson* ran aground, and its captain (Garfield's brother-in-law) committed suicide. Shortly thereafter, the *Bessie A. White* was grounded and lost off Moss Point, Long Island. The banks started to clamour for their money, and Garfield was forced to sell his businesses at a great loss. So ended the small financial empire of the Whites.

Throughout the first three decades of the twentieth century, attempts were made to use the scenery and wildlife of Alma Parish as a resource. Lakes were leased to clubs and sportsmen; some were even stocked with salmon, trout, bass and other fish. In 1920, an American boys' camp was established at Herring Cove, advertising overnight trips to Big Dam, Keyhole, Third Vault Falls, Goose River and Devil's Half Acre as well as woodcraft and watersports, camping in tepees, and voyages to Cape Blomidon and Ile Haute. Several cottages were built by Americans along the cliffs of Herring Cove, overlooking the small fishing weir that operated there. The Alma Hotel and Lake-View House (at Wolfe Lake) catered to hunting parties, and for the more adventurous, seven hunting camps were constructed back in the bush by two local men. Big game, the last resource to be exploited, was abundant. One story tells of a man shooting a good-sized doe and buck and a 300-pound bear, all on the same day.

Most of these enterprises were small, however, and could not pull the area out of its economic slump. In 1922, the mills and lands at Alma and Point Wolf were sold by Garfield White to Hollingsworth and Whitney, a pulp company. Uninterested in the land as anything more than a tree reserve, the company dismantled the mills. The era of river drives, lumber barons and shipbuilding was over forever in Alma Parish.

The next decade was one of depression and unemployment, and as local opportunities decreased, the exodus increased. Family names that had characterized the county for almost one hundred years suddenly started to appear in such far-away places as the United States and South Africa. "Along the road from Riverside to Herring Cove, one meets with many clearings, made by pioneers of a former generation, growing up into forest again," wrote one traveller; "Some farm houses are entirely deserted, and others are showing the dilapidation of age." A few local men were able to obtain employment by negotiating with Hollingsworth and Whitney for the right to cut timber on company property. Although these operations were small, they were vital to the struggling community. Portable mills were moved into the interior, and two small mills were built near the mouths of the Point Wolf and Upper Salmon rivers.

Despite the numerous economic upsets and shrinking size of the area's population, most people remained optimistic; historian Gilbert Allardyce has called Alma "the town that refused to conceive the possibility of its own death." Many people still thought the supply of trees inexhaustible, and the small lumber operations kept cutting and sawing. Other economic

Matthews Head field

Daylily

Lilac

avenues were explored: fox farming was tried by some, prospecting continued, and the big game hunting camps operated until declining moose populations caused the province to ban hunting.

THE NEW BRUNSWICK NATIONAL PARK
In the early thirties, the federal government started to search for a site for the proposed New Brunswick National Park. After considering four different locations, a portion of southern Albert County was selected, to preserve the beauty of the forests and shoreline, and to act as an economic stimulus to the surrounding communities. Only about fifty families

remained within Alma Parish when work on the park was started in 1948. Small farms and the settlements of Hastings, Alma West and Point Wolf were expropriated by the Government of New Brunswick. Former inhabitants, and in some cases their homes, were moved to sites outside the area. As a safety precaution, all remaining homes were razed. The land was turned over to the Government of Canada in 1948, and Fundy National Park was finally established, officially opening to the public in 1952. Allardyce has best summed up this change: "For over a century the settlers and lumbermen of the region had laboured to clear fields and exploit the woods. Now other men were coming to bring back the wilderness."

History has passed close by Fundy's shores, but great events have never touched them. Brooding high above the muddy waves, the park's cliffs have provided backdrops for a pageant of exploration, many attempts at settlement, and finally abandonment. The story has now come full circle, and the land will be wild forevermore.

A SUCCESSION STORY

The people who settled this land are long gone. Farms and fields that were tended for decades lie abandoned and are growing up as forest. Some farms were left just over thirty years ago, when the park was established, but many have lain fallow for more than twice that time.

Decade by decade the land returns to forest. At Hastings and Butland Settlement, where crops were planted and cows and sheep once grazed, field flowers and young spruce are now nibbled by deer and hare. Drained of nutrients by cropping and erosion, the thin soils are slow to recover. White lichens, yellow and orange hawkweeds, and scrubby alders all indicate the infertility of the old fields. That only these plants of poor soils can grow suggests the difficulty that faced farmers in this belt of "miserable spruce . . . fit to be inhabited only by wild beasts."

Boulders, painstakingly pried from the soil and piled in neat rows along the edges of fields, still mark the land. Removed from the soil to prevent damage to plough blades, the rocks were replaced by others each spring by the frost. An unending supply of broken stone lies beneath the soil and is worked to the surface by freezing and thawing. Heartbreaking to the farmer, these rock piles became sanctuaries. Here grew trees that were not removed by ploughing each year, now the oldest trees in the fields. Here grew blackberries and raspberries, trailing low over the rocks, and here grew boulder fern or hay-scented fern, fresh green and as fragrant as new-mown grass. Now the rocks provide homes for garter snakes, which overwinter deep below, hidden from the frost. In summer they lie placidly sunning themselves on the warm stones, golden eyes and red tongues flashing in the light, loath to flee even when approached.

Blueberries and cranberries spread rank stems across the ground, squeezing aside grasses and hawkweeds. Black ants, nippers but not stingers, pile mounds of earth and spruce needles ever higher as they dig their subterranean condominiums. Large circular mats of silver-green juniper hug the surface of the soil. Although soft looking, their spiny needles rival those of the thistle for making a deep impression. Fragrant waxy-blue berries cling to the branches of the female bushes, and once added flavour to settlers' food and scent to their candles. Ragged fringed-orchis, green adder's mouth and slender ladies-tresses, all small wild orchids, sprout from grassy patches. With them grows yellow-rattle, a parasite of grass, whose brown seed heads rattle in the wind.

Alders do well in old fields. Like clover, beans and peas, these shrubby trees have bacteria that live in nodules attached to their roots. The bacteria can remove nitrogen from the air in a form that is accessible to their roots. In this way alders can move quickly to colonize poor soils that will not support other trees. Their dead leaves and branches enrich the soil for plants yet to come.

White spruce, field spruce and cat spruce — all are names for the same tree with its white, wax-covered needles and unusual tomcat smell. Another tree that grows well in old fields, and has increased as the result of human activity, it is often found in rows, having seeded in the furrows of the last ploughing. Hidden deep in the shelter of its branches are the nests of white-throated sparrows, juncos, yellowthroats, and other field-loving birds.

Spruce that grow in the open maintain their wide-spreading lower branches for life. Forming the traditional conical Christmas tree shape, the branches remain even after the needles have long fallen off. These field-grown spruce are easily recognized in forest, and are a mark that the forest was probably field only a generation or so ago.

Grey rock piles, slowly being covered by mosses and ferns, snake through the forests of even-aged trees. Here and there glint pieces of broken glass and crockery, clues to the lives of those who once farmed this land. Pots, tin cans, pieces of stoves, and bits of harness and wagons moulder rusty red as they become soil. Quietly, the forest retakes the land that was wrested from it a century-and-a-half ago.

Foundation holes remain: dry fieldstones stacked carefully one atop the other, entrance ways and porch stones still awaiting the tread of feet. Faithfully, lilacs bloom, rhubarb patches and apple orchards produce their crops, and stray garden plants struggle to flower. More than one-third of a century has passed now since any of these once-treasured plants were tended. Each year the flowers are fewer, the foundations become harder to find, and the edge between field and forest grows more blurred.

Man has made his mark deep upon the face of the land, but in this small corner of New Brunswick, as in other national parks, wilderness will be allowed to return.

FUNDY NATIONAL PARK
— A USER'S GUIDE

I f you are planning a visit to Fundy, your most important consideration should be that precious commodity — time. Few of us are able to pay the same attention to detail as the naturalist-scientist Louis Agassiz, who once wrote, "I spent half the summer travelling, I got halfway across my back yard." All too often, one finds that time has fled, and a visit must end before it has really begun. You can "do" Fundy in a twenty-minute drive, but you will have wasted your time. A two- or three-day stay will give you a taste of what this park has to offer; however, to really start to know Fundy, you need at least a week.

This section of the guidebook is designed to help you in your orientation to the park and to present the full range of opportunities and activities available to you during your stay.

Six Special Places

To capture the essence of Fundy, a visitor should experience these six places:

The Edge of the Tide. Visit the expanse of Alma Beach at low tide; walk to the water's edge and let its slow rise nudge you back up to dry land. Be sure to see the same beach at both high and low tide to fully appreciate the water's rise.

Devil's Half Acre in the Fog. Rain, mist and dusk add an extra element of atmosphere to this haunting landscape. The trail is a good place to sit and look out over the bay. It is best enjoyed with a friend.

Caribou Plain Trail. This example of the flat uplands is a cross-section of softwood forest, bog and hardwoods — a flat and easy stroll.

The Coastal Trail. If you cannot manage the whole trail, at least visit the section from Matthews Head to the Squaws Cap lookout, a slice of coastal forest and rugged scenery.

The Point Wolfe Gorge. Old logging dam, mill pond, covered bridge,

Ancient pothole, now cut off from Broad River

precipitous cliffs, peregrine falcons, migrating salmon, riverside orchids, rare seacoast plants, trails and beach — these are the highlights of this historic and scenic valley.

The Broad River. The most impressive river scenery on the Upper Salmon River lies between the Forks Trail and Laverty Falls, a rugged hike.

INFORMATION

An *information kiosk* at Alma and another at Wolfe Lake provide maps, campground information, fishing permits and descriptions of interpretive events in both English and French. During the off-season, these services may be obtained at the park Administration Building in the Headquarters Area. Fundy is open to visitors every day of the year.

Bulletin Boards at the campgrounds, the park entrances and at other strategic locations throughout the park contain information about interpretation programs and events and some general park notices.

The Salt and Fir is a free, annually published park newspaper that contains articles about park projects, wildlife, visitor facilities and interpretation programs. A map of park trails with descriptions and average walking times forms one section, and another section lists local services and accommodations.

The Fundy Guild, Fundy National Park's non-profit co-operating association, operates two small bookstores, one at each information kiosk. For sale are books about the park, the natural and human history of the area, and other topics of local interest. Among other items, the Guild has produced a hiking map with trail profiles and descriptions, postcards and posters highlighting scenes in the park, a book of colour photographs and

Squaws Cap

text about the Bay of Fundy, and a children's activity book. The Guild also sponsors special events in the park and within the community of Alma.

ACCOMMODATIONS

Campgrounds. Fundy maintains nearly 700 campsites, including wilderness or backcountry sites. Headquarters, Point Wolfe, Chignecto and Wolfe Lake campgrounds are accessible by vehicle and all have kitchen shelters.

Twenty-nine fully serviced sites are available at Headquarters Campground and there are fifty-six electrically supplied sites at Chignecto. Except for Wolfe Lake, all other sites share centralized plumbing and each campground has, or is near, a playground. Headquarters and Point Wolfe have showers, and the latter also has a laundry. Headquarters Campground is a five-minute walk from an outdoor theatre where, from mid-June to the end of September, programs are given each evening. The golf course, tennis courts, swimming pool and the village of Alma are also nearby. Chignecto Campground is on the upland plateau, away from morning coastal fogs and just across the road from Chignecto Theatre, where programs are presented occasionally. Chignecto is the only campground with designated sites at which campfires are permitted. Firewood is available. Wolfe Lake is an unserviced lakeside campground. In addition to the individual campsites, there are four group tenting sites in the Micmac area with cookshelters, water and toilets, and a total capacity of 150 campers. These sites are available on a reservation basis.

Each of the campgrounds has a different character. Headquarters is on the coast and is relatively open. Three trails — Coastal, Whitetail and

Headquarters outdoor theatre

Devil's Half Acre — start nearby. Point Wolfe is also quite open and on the coast, less than five minutes walk from the cobble beach of Point Wolfe Cove. Four of the longer hiking trails depart from this area: Marven Lake, Goose River, Coppermine and Coastal. Chignecto Campground is well wooded. Whitetail and Kinnie Brook trails begin nearby.

Within the park are a motel and two sets of chalets. The chalets, only open during the summer, all have facilities for light housekeeping. Other accommodations are available in Alma and the surrounding area.

INTERPRETATION

One of the best ways to find out about the park is to take advantage of the interpretive services. Park interpreters, or naturalists, have an understanding and knowledge of the park's features which they share through programs, or less formally in conversation. Since the park is open throughout the year, interpretation programs of one sort or another are offered in every season, in both English and French. Summer is the busiest time, and evening programs often draw crowds of more than 400 people to the

PARKS CANADA

Kidstuff Program

theatres. Most events, however, are much more personal. Check at the park information booths or the bulletin boards for the description and times of events. Visitors who have recently entered New Brunswick from the deep south (Maine) or the far west (Quebec and Ontario) should check their watches against local time or they risk being one hour late for everything.

From late June to the end of September, evening programs are presented each night of the week at one or both of the park's outdoor theatres, starting at dusk and lasting about one hour. A program often consists of a slide-illustrated talk or a film about some aspect of Fundy or one of Canada's other national parks. It is always a good idea to bring insect repellent, and a blanket if the night feels cold.

Kidstuff, a program of activities for children between four and twelve years old, is presented during the summer, based on non-competitive games, art, drama and explorations. Each event reinforces the national park's conservation message.

Throughout the winter and spring there are no regularly scheduled events, but with advance notice, programs are available to visiting groups. The interpretation program also extends into local schools, where the need for preserving land as national parks is explained to the students so that they can better enjoy parks while helping to protect them.

WALKS AND HIKES

Park trails are grouped into three categories: day-use, front country and back country. This guide should help you select a walk suited to your interests and your pace. Please note that the time suggested for each trail is the average hiking time and allows for only brief stops. A topographic hiking map with trail descriptions and profiles can be bought at the information kiosks.

Linear trails are those that allow you to see the same piece of country from two different directions — coming and going. Loop trails take you from a parking lot into the woods and back out again without retracing your steps — not the sort of trail where you can hide that extra sweater in the bushes and hope to retrieve it on the way back.

Always check a map before starting on a hike, or better yet, bring the map with you. This will save you from any confusion about the length and difficulty of the hike and the destination of spur trails.

Trails are corridors into the wilderness, and there are more than 100 km of them to guide you into Fundy's special places.

Day-use trails are short, and do not climb any major hills. Walking time varies from fifteen minutes to two hours. Sneakers or comfortable shoes are appropriate footwear.

Dickson Brook is typical of Fundy's watercourses — swift and youthful, creating falls and rapids as it cuts vigorously into the highland plateau. *Dickson Falls Trail* leads to a tumbling waterfall, then follows the brook upstream. The path winds through trees downed by the effects of spruce budworm feeding, strong winds and shallow soils. Fast-growing birch, maple, balsam fir and raspberries crowd the sunlit spots, while ferns and spruce prefer the shade. Route: 1.0-km loop. Time: 30 minutes. Gentle grades and stairs. Access: parking and trailhead beside the Point Wolfe Road.

"This land is rocky, rough and [covered with] broken timber, it is called the Devil's Half Acre, and it is all rent in holes." (Surveyor's note, 1852) A tortured landscape of gaping holes, split rocks and collapsed trees awaits the hiker on the *Devil's Half Acre Trail*. Local legend blames the devil, but geologists speak of percolating water and sliding strata. Whatever your persuasion, you could fall into the crevasses, so a boardwalk guides you safely through. In the fog or after a rain, the trail is at its haunting best, although on a clear day you can gaze across the Bay of

Fundy to Nova Scotia. In winter, porcupines and raccoons den in the crevasses, and deer gather on the south-facing slope. Route: 1.1-km loop with interpretive signs. Small hills and steps. Time: 30 to 45 minutes. Access: turn off the Point Wolfe Road onto the Devil's Half Acre Road. Parking at trailhead, or walk the Coastal Trail from the swimming pool to the Devil's Half Acre Road, then turn left and follow the road to the trailhead.

You can stroll the *Shaded Maples Trail* over and over again, and feel all the changes of the seasons: warm and wet in spring; cool and quiet in summer; rustling and windy in autumn; brittle, stark and cold in winter. An offering to the senses, the trail wanders past rock outcrops with veins of milky quartz, over rivulets and through sunny glades. At least ten different kinds of ferns grow under the hardwood canopy. Route: 0.5-km loop with interpretive leaflet. Time: 15 to 30 minutes. Access: turn off the Point Wolfe Road and follow Maple Grove Road to the parking lot and trailhead.

An old wagon road slopes down to *Matthews Head,* where Tom and Ellen Matthews settled in 1865. The stone foundations of their farm buildings crumble as alder and spruce trees reclaim the cleared fields. Migrating birds sweep through the area in spring and fall, whereas deer, bobcat and porcupines reside there year-round. Route: linear trail, 3-km return, or link up to the Coastal Trail. Time: (return) 1½ to 2 hours. Access: parking lot 1.5 km along the Herring Cove Road; the trailhead is across the field.

In the 1890s a prospector home from the California gold rush discovered copper, gold and silver in quartz veins in this area. Prospect pits and a mine shaft yielded meagre and short-lived deposits. The *Coppermine Trail* retraces the road to the mine site. There eight men worked with picks, shovels and dynamite to remove the ore. Little remains: a tailings pile, a boiler blocking the mine shaft, and traces of blue-green copper carbonates (malachite and azurite) on rock fragments. The return trail offers a splendid panorama of the Fundy coast. Route: 4.4-km loop, best done counterclockwise for a gradual climb and steeper descent. Steep scramble to the mine opening (optional). Time: 2 to 2½ hours. Access: parking and trailhead across from Point Wolfe Campground.

Caribou Plain Trail is a cross-section through Fundy's forest — overgrown roads, tangled evergreen forest, leafy hardwoods and streamside alder thickets. But the highlight is the bog. A boardwalk that weaves among the spruces takes you out onto Caribou Plain — a living sponge of sodden peat moss, dwarf trees, insect-eating plants and native heaths. Two bog lakes harbour mink frogs, dragonflies, beavers and the occasional moose. Route: flat 3.4-km loop, with interpretive leaflet. Time: 1 to 1½ hours. Access: parking and trailhead beside Route 114, 10 km north of park Headquarters.

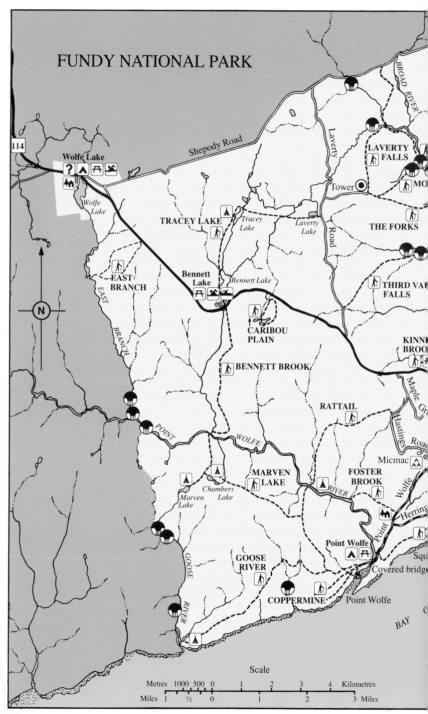

FUNDY NATIONAL PARK

Shepody Road

Wolfe Lake

Wolfe Lake

TRACEY LAKE

Tracey Lake

Laverty Lake

LAVERTY FALLS

Tower

MO

THE FORKS

EAST BRANCH

EAST BRANCH

Bennett Lake

Bennett Lake

THIRD VA FALLS

CARIBOU PLAIN

KINN BROO

BENNETT BROOK

RATTAIL

Maple Gr

Hastings Road

WOLFE

POINT

Chambers Lake

MARVEN LAKE

Marven Lake

Micmac

FOSTER BROOK

Wolfe

Point

Herring

Point Wolfe

GOOSE RIVER

GOOSE RIVER

COPPERMINE

Point Wolfe

Covered bridge

Squ

BAY

Scale

| Metres | 1000 | 500 | 0 | 1 | 2 | 3 | 4 | Kilometres |
| Miles | 1 | ½ | 0 | 1 | 2 | | 3 Miles |

LEGEND

Paved road	▬▬▬▬
Secondary road	▭▭▭▭
Unpaved road	═══
Trail	–[🚶]–
Warden station	🏠
Waterfall	🌊
Wilderness campsite	⛺
Information	?
Campground	⛺
Group campground	⛺⛺
Picnic area	🧺
Outdoor theatre	🎭
Exhibit	👤
Swimming	🏊
Pool	🏊P
Tennis	🎾
Golf	⛳
Boating	🛶
Services	S

Caribou Plain Trail

The *Cove Trail* leads from the parking lot at Herring Cove to a seacoast exhibit and viewing platform with a free telescope and then loops down to the beach. At the tip of the rocky headland is a small sea cave, accessible after a short scramble up the seaweed- and barnacle-encrusted rocks. Back on the upper beach, a step across a small brook leads to a stairway that climbs into the forest. Paralleling the gorge carved by the brook, the trail crosses over the top of a small waterfall, and returns to the parking lot. A side trail, part of the Coastal Trail, runs out to the top of Toms Head and overlooks the cove. Route: 1.0-km loop. Time: 30 minutes. Gentle grades and stairs. Access: Herring Cove parking lot.

Front country trails include medium-length routes (5 to 10 km) or short trails with major hills. Hiking time is two to four hours, so we suggest that you carry a lunch. Sturdy shoes, sneakers or light boots are suitable.

Tall red spruce, the trees that first attracted lumbermen to the Fundy coast, still grow along the *East Branch Trail*. The ancestors of these trees were felled with crosscut saw and axe, hauled to the East Branch River and sluiced downstream to the mill at Point Wolfe. The trail visits the disappearing remains of that era — the flush dam, log yard and the hauling road to the river. Old maple and birch mix with dark spruce and young balsam fir to form stands reminiscent of the original forest. Route: 5.5-km loop with interpretive signs. Level, with a gentle grade at the river. Time: 2 to 2½ hours. Access: parking and trailhead beside Route 114, 15.7 km north of park Headquarters.

Third Vault Brook boasts the tallest waterfall in the park (16 m), and the pool at its base is probably the coolest. Despite several rocky spots, *Third Vault Trail* is flat until it nears the edge of the brook valley. Stairs lessen the pitch as the path winds down to a tributary stream. Twenty metres upstream Third Vault Brook plunges into a deep, round pool. Mist from the falls bathes the rocky sides of the valley, nourishing the lush growth of mosses and tiny ferns that cling to cracks and ledges. Route: linear trail, 7.4-km return. Time (return): 3 to 3½ hours. Access: turn off Route 114 onto Laverty Road. Trailhead and parking lot 1 km down the road.

The focus of *Kinnie Brook Trail* is a valley — steep walls, lichen-encrusted boulders, and a disappearing stream. The trail skirts the upper edge of the valley before descending a long flight of stairs to the stream bed. In the spring, water laps at the foot of the stairs; at other times it seeps through the gravel to flow beneath the surface. This is locally called "the Strainer." A scramble downstream through a dry gulch reveals the brook's resurgence. Upstream, lush stands of ostrich fern, cow parsnip, red osier dogwood and sensitive fern crowd the floodplain. Gray jays frequent the trailhead and picnic area. Route: linear trail, 2.4-km return. Time (return): 1½ to 2 hours. Access: trailhead and parking at picnic area 4.5 km north of park headquarters.

The *Whitetail Trail* rambles over the south-facing slopes west of park headquarters in a prime area for seeing deer. They gather here in winter and summer to feed, to rest, to court, and when the snow is deep, to yard. Starting at Chignecto Campground, the path crosses overgrown fields and offers glimpses of the bay before easing down a long hill beside a small ravine to the Headquarters Area. Joining the Coastal Trail at the swimming pool, a ridge-top walk with seaward views carries you to Herring Cove. Climbing up and over the ridge, you gain a view of the forest spreading from the road below, up and over the opposite hillside. The path drops into Dickson Brook valley, where hard-luck beavers are cutting young hardwoods almost as quickly as they sprout. The trail crosses the Point Wolfe Road, then begins a final climb through ferns and hardwoods to Chignecto Campground. Route: 7.3-km open loop with equal numbers of strenuous climbs and steep descents. The inclusion of a section of the Coastal Trail completes a loop of 10.4 km. The clockwise circuit is the easiest. Time (loop): 4¼ to 5 hours. Access: 4 trailheads with parking —

Kinnie Brook Trail, descent to valley floor

FUNDY GUILD

Third Vault Falls Trail

Point Wolfe River estuary

behind the clubhouse in Headquarters Area, at the entrance to Chignecto Campground, on the Point Wolfe Road 3 km from Headquarters, and at Herring Cove.

Foster Brook Trail provides the fastest and easiest access to a river valley in the park. For most of the trail the walking is easy, through cool shaded forest. Towards its end, the path slopes steeply to the Point Wolfe River, and the forest merges with the floodplain vegetation — red maples, yellow birch, ferns and, in early summer, carpets of wildflowers. This river is once again the home of Atlantic salmon, restored through a stocking program and alteration of the dam at the river mouth. Route: linear trail, 3.8-km return. Time (return): 1½ to 2 hours. Access: trailhead and parking behind warden station on Point Wolfe Road. An alternative and slightly more difficult return is along the banks of the Point Wolfe River to the covered bridge and from there by road to the trail parking lot — another 1½ to 2 hours.

Sea cliffs, lapping waves and scenes that carry your gaze out over the bay help to create a memorable hike along Fundy's *Coastal Trail*. From Headquarters you climb to a ridge where tree roots grasp the rocky hillside and bracing winds challenge their hold. The path runs along the ridge past a series of yawning mossy chasms, an extension of the Devil's Half Acre area, then drops down to a picnic site and beach at Herring Cove. The trail to Point Wolfe rises from the cove to a ridge-top view of rolling hills and eroded coastline. It then wanders through coastal forest, emerging at headlands such as Matthews Head and hugging the cliff tops above lonely Squaws Cap. In the last 2 km, the trail draws back from the coast and crosses a final ridge before descending a switchback to Point Wolfe. Route: linear trail, in 2 sections: Headquarters to Herring Cove 3.3 km (one way), Herring Cove to Point Wolfe 5.6 km (one way). Time (one way): 4½ to 5 hours. Access: 3 trailheads with parking — on Point Wolfe Road near the swimming pool, at Herring Cove and at Point Wolfe, east of the bridge.

Backcountry trails include longer hikes or short trails over more difficult terrain. Those with steep hills will take more time than their distance suggests. You should carry a lunch and wear suitable hiking footwear. On long linear trails with road access at either end, you might arrange to hike out with a group and to leave a vehicle at both ends.

Primitive camping is allowed only at designated sites. For any overnight stay at a backcountry campsite it is necessary to register at an information kiosk or at the Point Wolfe Campground kiosk, both as a safety precaution and to reserve campsites. Sites are allocated without charge on a first-come, first-served basis. All wilderness sites have hearths and a supply of wood, but for safety and conservation, fires should be kept small. New

Laverty Falls

backcountry campsites and trail connections are under construction, with more planned for completion within the next few years. It is advisable to ask about them at an information kiosk, or even better, to speak to a warden or interpreter about your planned hike. Either one will be able to give you up-to-date information about your route, suggest side trips and points of interest, and note any hazards.

Just over an hour's walk from the Laverty fire tower, Laverty Brook pours over a broad rock face to form a curtain waterfall. *Laverty Falls Trail* descends steadily to the brook through mixed forest and hardwood stands. Spruce trees frame the falls, and tiny insect-eating sundews nestle on rock ledges. The best view is from downstream, where boulders provide poolside seats. Route: linear trail, 4.6-km return with a gradual slope. Alternative trail from the Shepody Road, linear, relatively flat, 5.2-km return. Time: 2 to 2½ hours, tower to falls (return); 3 to 3½ hours, tower to Shepody Road (one way). Access: turn off Route 114 onto Laverty Road. Parking and trailhead at the fire tower. Second trailhead 2.5 km east of Laverty Road–Shepody Road junction.

Along the *Upper Salmon River Trail* the character of Fundy's rivers unfolds — tranquil in the headwaters, steep-walled and spectacular in the midsections, and shallow and rocky near the coast. (In 1985, only the upper section of this trail was complete. It will eventually reach to the river's mouth, connecting with the Forks, Third Vault and Black Hole trails.) Along the floodplain of Laverty Brook the trail is shady, the tread soft and the plant growth lush. Downstream on the Broad River, alder thickets crowd the old headpond above Big Dam. Below the remains of the dam, the gradient steepens, the valley narrows and the river sluices

Moosehorn Trail

through a rock channel into a long, deep and inviting pool. The path hugs the valley wall, but river enthusiasts may prefer to scramble and rock hop over the chutes, rapids and potholes. Route: linear trail, 2.7 km. Time: one hour (one way). Access: from the end of the Moosehorn or Laverty trails. The most comfortable way to walk this loop is to begin on the Moosehorn, thereby descending rather than climbing the steepest slope.

The *Moosehorn Trail,* named after a logger's portage, provides access to the wild midsection of the Broad River. The path weaves through mixed forest and overgrown clearings to the upper edge of the valley. Beside the trail, a small stream plunges down the valley wall to the river. The trail does likewise, but less precipitously. Route: linear trail, 4.2-km return, strenuous. Time: (return) 2½ to 3 hours. Access: turn off Route 114 onto Laverty Road. Trail begins at the Laverty fire tower.

From the Laverty fire tower, the *Forks Trail* heads downslope to the confluence of the Broad and Fortyfive rivers. On a sandy ridge the trail breaks out of the trees and lends a view of the valley before switchbacking to the water's edge. In front of you, Broad River spills into the Bathtub pool. From the other side, the Fortyfive River invites you upstream to a falls and canyon that the loggers dubbed the Matchfactory. Down the valley, gathering its tributaries, the Upper Salmon River speeds towards the bay. Route: linear trail, branching from the Moosehorn Trail 180 m from the entrance, 6-km return, strenuous. Time (return): 3 to 3½ hours. Walking along the river is slow and difficult. Access: turn off Route 114 onto Laverty Road. Parking and trailhead at the fire tower.

The Forks Trail

In late summer and autumn, Atlantic salmon rest in the Black Hole pool before moving upstream to spawn. The *Black Hole Trail* leads down an old road to this pool on the Upper Salmon River. Shaded by a canopy of hardwoods, the trail is an easy walk until it reaches the edge of the river valley. There, with the sound of the rapids below, it drops sharply to the river and the wardens' log cabin. This is a beautiful hike at any time of the year, but especially so in the fall. Route: linear trail, 11-km return. Some sections are wet, some are rocky. Time (return): 4 to 4¼ hours. Access: parking and trailhead on the Fortyfive Road, west of Lake Brook.

The old cart track to the tiny settlement of Goose River provides the route for the *Goose River Trail*. The road winds through coastal forest, cresting hills that offer glimpses of the bay and dropping into the valleys of Mile Brook and Schoolhouse Creek. Ghosts of the old community linger: gooseberry bushes, rock foundations, small fields becoming forest, and the old school yard — silent and overgrown. The sight of Goose River greets you from the last hilltop, a wide sand and gravel bar arches across the river mouth, sheltering a pocket of salt marsh in its lee. Backcountry camping is permitted here, and day-hikers can explore the beach and river before heading back. Route: linear trail, 16-km return. Time (return): 4½ to 5 hours. Access: parking and trailhead across from Point Wolfe Campground.

Marven Lake Trail reaches to the shores of Marven and Chambers lakes, where backcountry campers may wake to the splashing of a moose or beaver feeding. In the heat of the day the bass drones of bullfrogs boom

107

across the water. The shallow lakes are dark with acids from their boggy margins, but native brook trout dart beneath the surface, feeding on the many small insects that live there. The old road is wide, and the walking is easy. The trail links with the steeper Rattail and Bennett Brook trails to provide access to the Point Wolfe River. Route: linear trail, branching north from the Goose River Trail, 16-km return. Time (return): 4½ to 5 hours. Access: parking and trailhead across from Point Wolfe Campground.

Old farmsteads with a panoramic view of the bay mark the beginning of *Rattail Trail*. From a country lane, the trail enters the forest and traces a logger's road along the hardwood ridge. Sidling into the valley of Rattail Brook, the path drops to the Point Wolfe River and emerges beside the swift boulder-strewn shallows and a backcountry campsite. This can be the turnaround point of the hike or the start of another section. By fording the stream, you can join the second half of the trail 100 m upstream. It climbs through tall red spruce to the Marven Lake Trail — an alternative route to the backcountry campsites, or a quick way back to Point Wolfe. Route: linear trail, 5.4 km one way, another 1.5 km to Marven Lake Trail, steep. Time (one way): 2 to 2½ hours, another 45 minutes to Marven Lake Trail. Access: trailhead and parking 2 km from Route 114 along Hastings Road.

For the most of its length, *Bennett Brook Trail* is an old logging road where hikers can stroll side by side and, in season, sample wild strawberries or raspberries. The trail parallels the brook along the upper edge of its valley, but reserves access to it until the end. From a bluff 150 m above the Point Wolfe River, the path ducks into the trees and winds down to a quiet pool at the mouth of Bennett Brook. Fifty metres up the Point Wolfe River the trail continues — rising up the rocky, frost-shattered hillside. As you climb, glimpses of the river valleys far below give way to a spectacular vista of Fundy's highlands. Route: linear trail, 5 km one way, another 1.8 km to Marven Lake Trail. Gentle grades, except for steep climbs on both sides of the river. Time (one way): 1½ to 2 hours, another hour to Marven Lake Trail. Access: parking and trailhead at Bennett Lake.

The *Tracey Lake Trail* links four small lakes that nestle in the poorly drained northern section of the park. Moose roam nearby and beavers find food and shelter in the shallow lakes and nearby streams. Crossing coniferous woods, the path skirts the shore of Bennett Lake and follows a stream to the edge of Tracey Lake where there are three campsites. Black spruce and pitcher plants grow on the lakeshore. The trail continues to Laverty Lake over gentle knolls with several wet spots. Route: linear trail, Bennett to Laverty, 13.8-km return; Bennett to Tracey, 8.2-km return. Time: (return) 2 to 2½ hours Bennett to Tracey, 2 hours Tracey to Laverty. Access: 2 trailheads with parking — at Bennett Lake and at Laverty Lake, 4.25 km from Route 114 along Laverty Road.

In the Backcountry

There is usually no need to carry water while hiking in the park. Fresh springs trickle into the streams and rivers all along their courses, and most are safe for drinking. Drink only from those well away from trails. It is always best to take water from a small fresh source rather than from a large one; at least you know where the water has been.

Handfuls of berries can be picked and eaten on the spot, but the collecting of large quantities is frowned upon. The berries are there, after all, for the use of birds, insects and mammals, not humans. The digging of roots, breaking of branches and picking of leaves and flowers is illegal within a national park. No living off the land here, except for bona fide park inhabitants — those with tails.

There are few really dangerous animals in the park. Raccoons sometimes break into tents and packs while searching for food, and may bite those who try to feed them. Uncommon and wary, bobcats, coyotes and bears are predators, but not of humans. Nesting hawks sometimes dive-bomb people who approach their nests, but always give plenty of loud warning. As long as you respect the privacy of animals, especially those with young, and do not try to approach too closely for their comfort, you should have no trouble. Two animals to avoid, should you be lucky enough to see them, are bears — especially cubs — and moose during the autumn rutting season. Most wild animals go out of their way to avoid you; but always remember that "wild" means "unpredictable."

Poison ivy grows in the park in a few very restricted locations along river banks and on cliffs. If you plan a hike and are particularly sensitive to this plant, ask for exact locations to shun.

When hiking off the trails along a river, it sometimes becomes necessary to climb a hillside to avoid a difficult section of bank. Do not place too much trust in roots and small trees as handholds, since many will come away in your hands. Test each hold carefully before putting your weight on it. Because many riverside and hillside mosses, ferns and trees are only tenuously attached to the rocks on which they grow, they are very sensitive to disturbance. Please think of the plants and what they will look like to people that use the route after you. Heavy foot damage can take years to repair.

When planning a hike along the rivers, it is important to check the water level. Spring freshet makes them impassable for a week or two in April, and they remain swollen for about three days after a heavy rain. During most of the summer there is enough bank for comfortable walking, and when the water is low it is possible to rock-hop right down the middle of many streams.

Some bogs contain flarks — places where the living skin of moss has died and a wet brown scar has appeared on the surface of the bog. These

Young bull moose

are *extremely dangerous,* since anyone or anything that steps into them will have a difficult time getting back out. Wet, decaying peat-moss acts like quicksand; there are few roots and stems to hold on to, and certainly no rocks to grab. One flark in Caribou Plain bog has captured two full-grown moose in the last decade — two that we know about. These dangerous peaty wallows are easy to avoid: if you must cross a bog, keep well away from any patches that look wet.

When walking or hiking along a section of bayshore, always be aware of the tides. Tide times are posted at various places throughout the park, and tables are available at the Fundy Guild book store. If you do get trapped in a cove by the rising tide, the best thing to do is find a safe ledge on the rock as far above the upper limit of brown and green seaweeds as possible, then just sit it out. After a couple of hours' wait, the tide will drop and you can resume your walk. Because the rocks are loose and crumbly in many places along the shore, you will be much safer waiting than trying to scramble up.

Pit privies are provided at some trailheads and at backcountry campsites. Should you find yourself caught short, move well off the trail, far away from any brook, spring or other water source, and dig a small hole. Dispose of paper in the hole and cover carefully. This is the only case where the pack-in, pack-out rule is not enforced, so please help to keep hiking pleasant for those who follow you.

Whether you are on a short hike, picnicking or camping overnight, remember to leave each place that you visit as clean as, or cleaner than, it was when you arrived. Think of this as your park, not someone else's.

What to Wear

The soils of southern Albert County are thin, and along river valleys the ferns, mosses and trees cling to almost-bare rock. Trails in the park are seldom steep, and even where they are, the footing is firm. Heavy lug-soled boots are unnecessary here. Damage done by these boots to trails, woodland soils, tree roots and moss carpets can take years to heal. Light walking shoes or sturdy sneakers are appropriate footwear for most trails; on very wet days rubber boots will do for short walks. There is no scree; no poisonous snakes or scorpions skulk in wait for the unwary; no spike-like cactus spines or shards of razor-sharp rocks protrude. For the most part, Fundy's trails are benign.

On the beaches, rubber boots or old sneakers are the best footwear — something that will keep you dry and protect you from mud, or that will dry quickly. Beware of seaweed patches — stepping on them too quickly could lead to your downfall.

Dress for the weather, and carry something warm to change into. These two rules will serve you well if you plan to hike in the park. Whatever the weather is doing now, it is bound to change before your hike is over, so be prepared. If you get too warm, it is always easy to cool down, but if you get cold and have no extra clothing, your hike will be miserable. A light nylon windbreaker that can be crumpled into a daypack or worn around the waist is generally sufficient in summer. It will keep flies off, and save you from getting scratched by branches. Nylon rain pants are also very useful. A safety kit of knife, whistle, compass, matches, bandages, emergency blanket and so on is worth its weight if you plan a long hike.

Many people find shorts and T-shirts too cool for wear along the coast, though they may be comfortable on the plateau. It is worth remembering that there is almost always a cool breeze on the beach, even if the parking lot air is calm and warm. Take that sweater or windbreaker with you; you need it more than the car does.

If you are hiking off-trail along one of the rivers you will be forced to get your feet wet, except at extremely low water. Wear your boots to cross, or change into sandals, sneakers or a thick pair of socks. Do not try to cross barefoot. Alga-covered rocks make treacherous footing, and you will need all of the traction that you can get. The cold water also makes it hard to feel the bottom, and lacerated feet are difficult to walk on. Take care of yourself and your visit will be more enjoyable.

Off-trail backpacking in the park is a lot easier with a frameless pack. Alder swales and dense tangles of second-growth spruce make passage almost impossible for anyone wearing a frame. Windthrown spruce and fir, especially in narrow ravines and stream valleys, must be climbed over and scrambled under, and frame packs have an uncanny ability to reach out and grab things.

RECREATION

For those who have enjoyed the trails and want a change of pace, or for those who prefer a more sedentary recreation, Fundy has a wide range of facilities:

The park's nine-hole *golf course,* with its first tee atop a grassy cliff and with a felt-like putting green that most billiard tables would be proud of, attracts many visitors. It also attracts a lot of wildlife. Deer graze on the grass and feed on the apple blossoms and fruit in an old orchard that is part of the course. Groundhogs are trying to increase the course to eighteen holes. Raccoons and porcupines can often be seen crossing the greens, and an occasional bear ambles by at night looking for berries, apples and grubs. Animal watchers must keep in mind that this *is* a golf course and they must follow the appropriate etiquette — stay clear of the players and out of their line of fire. A fee is charged for use of the course, and clubs and carts can be rented at the pro shop. Season passes are available. A licensed restaurant/clubhouse with free showers overlooks the course.

It is important to remember that the consumption of alcoholic beverages is *prohibited* in *all* areas of the park except at the restaurant and at individual campsites.

Across the road from the clubhouse are three *tennis courts,* a *lawn bowling green, swings and slides* and a *baseball diamond.* For those who like to swim in salt water but who do not relish the mud or invigorating chill of the bay, a *swimming pool* at Cannontown Beach warms and filters bay water into a more civilized form. Daily, weekly or season tickets may be purchased. Change rooms and showers are provided.

Facilities for the handicapped. Some facilities accessible to handicapped visitors are available; telephone the park for more information.

OTHER ACTIVITIES

For years Fundy has been thought of as a quiet little family park with swings and slides for the children and a golf course to keep their parents out of trouble. Recent work on the trail system has made the rugged backcountry much more accessible, and this upgrading is attracting hikers and backpackers. Between the extremes of relaxed lawnbowling and golf and the vigorous pleasures of rockhopping and orienteering there are many other activities for which the park is admirably suited.

Sitting and watching is a much underrated pastime. Once the private sport of authors, artists and the elderly, this activity is now in vogue with vacationers of all sorts. National parks offer the best outdoor sitting and watching opportunities available. Not only are there animals and plants, the sea and the clouds to observe but also a bearable number of people and cars to add variety. Quiet forest groves, riverside rocks, sheltered beaches and the expanse of lawn in the Headquarters bowl are traditionally favoured locations. You are not wasting time, you are stretching it.

Photography is the technical branch of the sport of sitting and watching. The photographer tries to capture some of his or her quiet observations on film. In this way the experience can be relived at home when winter weather makes the outdoors less comfortable. Fundy offers unlimited possibilities to photographers, especially with the effects of its changeable weather conditions.

Bicycling is a difficult activity in the park because of Fundy's roller-coaster topography. The best cycling stretches are the Point Wolfe Road and campground roads, especially the old Chignecto South Campground. Quiet bikers are often rewarded with close views of wildlife. Chignecto South is usually free of cars and makes a great bike trail for children.

All-terrain vehicles are prohibited within the park.

Numerous old fields, large grassed areas and a lack of hydro lines make the park ideal for *kite flying,* especially if one is using a steerable kite that requires lots of sky and soft ground for crash landings. "Go fly a kite" is not an insult here — it's an invitation.

Swimming at Fundy comes in a variety of flavours: chilled, salty Bay of Fundy water, a pool in the Headquarters Area that uses filtered and heated bay water, and the sparkling fresh water of rivers and lakes. The rivers and lakes offer the most varied and pleasant swimming, though river water is often kindly referred to as "bracing." Bennett and Wolfe lakes have small beaches with unsupervised swimming in the warm shallows. The larger rivers abound with quiet secluded pools, some almost 6 m deep.

Swimming in rivers can be hazardous when the water is high. Do not enter pools that show a strong current, do not swim alone, and never dive head first into any pool. Attire is optional.

Fishwatching. Birdwatchers, stargazers, people watchers and even

Boating at Bennett Lake

clock watchers visit the park each summer, but rarely does one meet a fishwatcher. Many visitors keep aquariums, or enjoy persuing the coolers of their local fishmarket, but few have ever had the opportunity to watch fish in their natural environment.

Instead of binoculars and checklists, fishwatchers generally carry a day-pack stuffed with a lunch, a towel and a diving mask, perhaps even a snorkel and fins. Polarized sunglasses give a clear view of fish on the river bottoms by cutting out sparkle and reflections.

Once fish are spotted, the enthusiast watches quietly from the shore or, if especially hardy, slips into the water with mask and snorkel. There fish can be watched from the shallows as they rest, feed and school about. As colourful as birds, trout quickly adapt to the presence of a person in their midst, but the large silver salmon remain wary. Water magnifies the size of fish by about one-third, so excited descriptions should be taken with a grain of salt by those on shore. The only requirements for fish watching are patience and tolerance for cold water, and the only rules are that fish must not be molested, and that no attempt may be made to catch them. These rules are enforced.

Birdwatching. Officially, 238 species of birds have been seen in Fundy, although only about 100 species actually nest here. A good cross-section of habitats and thus of the park's bird life may be obtained by visiting four locations:

1 The Headquarters Area around MacLaren Pond and the trees and shrubs at the outdoor theatre attract unusual birds during migration.
2 Coppermine Trail provides a sample of coastal softwood forest and shoreline — a good place to watch for warblers, loons and seaducks such as common eiders and scoters. Nearby is the peregrine falcon release site.

Magnolia warbler   *Boreal chickadee*

3 Caribou Plain Trail twists through a semi-boreal forest of spruce and bog and then passes into a hardwood grove. Watch for black-backed woodpeckers and gray jays in the woods and rusty blackbirds at the boggy lakes.

4 The hardwood forest is represented by the Shaded Maples Trail. In season, numerous northern warblers and thrushes call from the cover of trees and ferns.

Some birds that visitors often ask about: the boreal chickadee is seen here mainly in winter; the three-toed woodpecker is rare but sometimes is seen in mature or budworm-killed softwood stands, as at Laverty Lake; spruce grouse are very rarely seen, and puffins are found only at the mouth of the bay, never at the park.

Up-to-date information can usually be obtained from park staff.

Boating. Canoes and rowboats may be rented at Bennett Lake during the summer, and private boats can be used on this and other park lakes. Motors are illegal. Wind surfing and small sailboats are allowed, if you can scare up enough wind to move them. Park rivers are not suited to boating.

Fishing. Fishing in national parks is not a right but a carefully regulated privilege. At present, regulations differ for the various park rivers and lakes. A national park licence is required, and with it comes a pamphlet that explains where, when and how you can fish legally. More information can be obtained from park staff. The rules affecting Atlantic salmon are particularly subject to change as the provincial and federal governments co-operate to save the dwindling stocks.

Scenic Drives. Maple Grove and Hastings are one-way gravel roads that form a loop. Maple Grove Road rises up a steep hillside through overarching maples to the spruce-covered plateau and then joins the Hastings Road and returns towards the coast through old fields, giving a splendid view of forest and coast. This is a fine route for deer watching. It is not suited to trailers or campers.

Laverty Road is a trip over gently rolling hills that reveals the mosaic of Fundy's forest. In places, the hardwoods close overhead and the road winds through a leafy, green tunnel. You might stroll down to Laverty Lake where pitcher plants grow along the boggy shore, and moose and beaver sometimes feed in the evening. A wonderful drive in late October when fall colours are at their best. Return to Route 114 via the boundary roads: the Fortyfive, which crosses a covered bridge, or the Old Shepody, one of the oldest roads in the province.

Dogs and Cats. Family pets are allowed in the park, but must *always* be kept under control, preferably on a leash. This is not only to protect animals and people from your pet but also to protect your pet from itself. Fundy National Park has a lot of porcupines. Many dogs enjoy chasing after porcupines. Porcupines don't run. The closest veterinary clinic is in Moncton/Riverview.

AROUND AND ABOUT
Fundy National Park is located in New Brunswick's smallest county — Albert. Most visitors to the park arrive by Route 114, joining it either at Penobsquis (near Sussex) or at Moncton. It is not a main highway but a scenic road that almost encircles the county, twisting through towns and villages, some of which date from Acadian settlement in the late 1700s.

Moncton is the home of a number of attractions, the largest of which is the Petitcodiac River. At low tide, the river is almost drained and its reddish water trickles like liquid mud. Wide banks stretch glistening and glutinous on either side of its channel. The weird beauty of this carved and gulleyed mud is almost impossible to photograph. Reflecting the blue sky of day, the orange of evening and a rainbow of city lights at night, it adds a surreal dimension to this essentially flat city.

Twice each day, a tidal bore advances up the Petitcodiac River. Created by the rising tide in the bay, the bore represents the advancing front of the tide's rise in the river. Moncton has a Bore Park for those who wish to watch the wave. More interesting perhaps than the bore itself is the speed with which the river swells and fills after the bore has passed. The brick-red water pours into the branching mud gullies, rises on their banks and then floods out across the mud flats to completely inundate them, finally stretching from shore to shore like a muddy lake. Viewed at low tide, then again at high, the river is totally different. Tidal bores occur in many rivers around the head of the bay, and local newspapers list their times of arrival.

At Stoney Creek a gas and oil field has been in production since 1909.

The field is not open to the public, but pumps and tanks can be seen from the road and from the steam railway that leaves Hillsborough.

Fourteen kilometres from Moncton, the town of Hillsborough was once the home of a large gypsum plant, hence the white crumbly rock everywhere; it is now New Brunswick's major railway centre — for steam engines, that is. The Salem-Hillsborough Railway operates tours throughout the spring, summer and autumn over 16 km of track. Another historical aspect of Hillsborough is the annual Steeves family reunion, held to commemorate one of the founding families of the town. One of their descendants, William Henry Steeves, was a Canadian Father of Confederation, and his home has become a museum in the town.

Old houses with extensive "gingerbread" ornamentation and widow's-walks and captain's-watches on their roofs overlook the remains of wharves that line the Petitcodiac River. These large homes are reminders of the lumbering, trading and shipbuilding that once brought prosperity to the county. One-room schoolhouses, abandoned railway lines and deserted fields are signs of the less prosperous years that followed. Carefully maintained covered bridges, restored houses and extensive wildlife conservation areas preserve the historic and natural assets of this small county.

Just outside Hillsborough, near the village of Albert Mines, are roadside mounds and quarries containing white, banded, pink and yellow gypsum as well as clear grey crystals. The easily eroded gypsum has created a karst topography behind the village, with sinkholes, caves and disappearing streams. On this calcium-rich rock grow a variety of Arctic plants not found elsewhere in the province. Albertite, a hard shiny-black, tar-like mineral, which was mined nearby in the late 1800s, was named after the county. Aside from one other location in New Brunswick, it is found nowhere else in the world. Its discoverer, Abraham Gesner, also invented kerosene (1852).

At the village of Hopewell Cape is a beautifully preserved turn-of-the-century courthouse and the Albert County Museum, or "Museum in a Gaol." The 120-year-old cells contain reminders of a grisly nineteenth-century murder and the scratchings left by prisoners marking off their time. Another building houses antique farm implements.

Farther down the road, a white picket fence surrounds the overgrown birthplace of R. B. Bennett, Canadian Prime Minister from 1930 to 1935.

A few kilometres farther, at The Rocks Provincial Park, bay water has eroded soft conglomerate rock into gigantic sculptures. By enlarging cracks between huge blocks of bedrock, tidal water has created grottoes. As the caves erode further, they join and their roofs collapse, leaving towering stone islands balanced on thin columns. Trees, small plants and the soil in which they grew sit precariously atop most of the urn-shaped rocks.

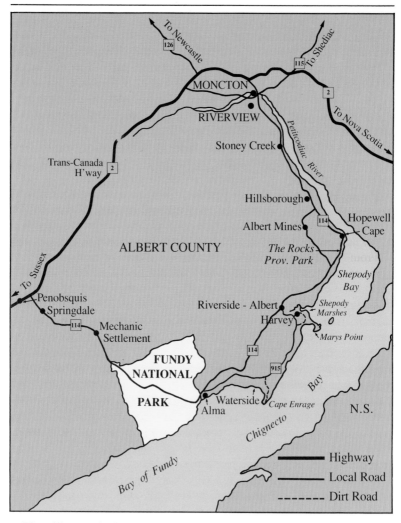

The villages of Riverside-Albert and Harvey lie on either side of extensive dyked marshland. Acadians settled this area in the 1690s, calling it Chipoudie. Few signs remain of their occupation, but the salt marshes that they dyked and cultivated are maintained and cropped to this day, and still bear the name "Shepody marshes." Replacing the Acadians' wooden clapper valves — *aboiteaux* — a tidal dam at Harvey keeps salt water off the marshes and allows fresh water to drain. Most of the land is used as community pasture or for hay. Albert and Harvey were prosperous villages at the turn of the century and contain a number of fine old homes as well as a huge wooden school that was built in 1905. The Albert County Fair, held in Albert each autumn, has a parade, midway, agricultural

Salt marshes rim the upper bay

exhibitions and contests. The closest bank to the park is in Albert.

From Albert to Alma, Route 114 runs beside the Germantown marshes, some sections of which are cultivated and others flooded. Maintained by the Canadian Wildlife Service, the flooded portions are protected to encourage waterfowl nesting. Geese, ducks and a wide variety of other animals feed and live in these new freshwater marshes. One part of a marsh where circular trenches have been dug to provide nesting islands for birds looks like a flying-saucer spaceport. From here to the park, the road runs through forest along what was once a railway route on which Alma was truly the end of the line.

The alternative route from Albert to Alma and the park is along Route 915, which passes through the village of Harvey and runs through rugged farmland to the coast. A side road leads to a portion of the Shepody National Wildlife Area called Marys Point, a small island joined to the mainland at low tide by a sand isthmus. From July to October, flocks of shorebirds land there to rest and feed as they migrate from Arctic nesting grounds to winter quarters in Central and South America. The vast mudflats of Shepody Bay provide food in the form of worms and tiny crustaceans to fuel the birds on their 4600-km non-stop southward journey. A trail leads from the parking lot to a small deck on the beach from where the birds can be observed without disturbing them.

About 12 km from Harvey along Route 915 is a narrow gravel road that leads to pocket coves and beaches and the Cape Enrage lighthouse. Farther along this route, Waterside marsh is a good place to watch ducks, herons and shorebirds. Seaward of the marsh, a sandy beach extends 2.5 km to Red Head, a tall sea stack of soft red Triassic sandstone. On the other side of this rock, the sand stretches for another 2.5 km and is known as Dennis Beach. At low tide, the beach is .5 km wide, a long flat walk to the water's edge.

Alma, the service centre for the park, is the only working port in Albert County, and has a year-round population of about 350. During the summer, motels and a hotel operate in the village, and bed-and-breakfast facilities are open in the surrounding area. Only the bed-and-breakfasts remain open in winter. Information about these facilities is available from Tourism New Brunswick, P.O. Box 12345, Fredericton, N.B., E3B 5C3. Two grocery stores, a snack bar, a recreation centre, two service stations, a roller skating–ice skating rink and a post office are open all year. In addition, restaurants, souvenir shops, a bake shop and a laundromat operate during the summer. In season, fresh lobster, scallops and fish are available. The Alma Jubilee is a festival held each July first weekend, with parades, a boat race, a bonfire, contests, games and other activities.

Linking the Trans-Canada Highway (at Penobsquis) and Fundy National Park, Route 114 traces valley bottoms through farmland and forest, climbs for views of wooded valleys and hillsides, crisscrosses branches of the Kennebecasis and Pollett rivers, and winds past blueberry fields and jack-pine plantations. Houses cluster along the route at the settlements of Springdale, South Branch and Mechanic Settlement, the latter founded in 1843 by one hundred out-of-work mechanics and one hundred labourers from Saint John. At Springdale, sparkling water gushes from the hillside through summer's droughts and winter's cold to swell verdant moss-lined brooks. Closer to the park, commercial blueberry fields are burned over in the spring and harvested in late summer; in autumn they blaze into red, maroon and purple patchworks that blanket the hillsides.

Just before Route 114 enters the park it intersects Old Shepody Road, once the only inland connection between the port of Saint John and communities along the upper bayshore. For over two hundred years it provided access to the interior, and became a ribbon of settlements and small villages. Poor land and poorer job prospects led to its almost complete abandonment in the last hundred years, and now it serves mainly as a logging road. About 18 km of this road are within the northern boundary of the park.

WINTER IN FUNDY

National Parks do not hibernate during the winter. As snow begins to fall, tobogganers visit the hills in Fundy's Headquarters Area, skaters flock to MacLaren Pond, and park wardens set trails for use during the coming cross-country ski season. Fifty kilometres of trail are groomed each winter from short beginners' trails to more challenging trails with long hills. Skiers can use these routes or break their own trails on snow-covered roadways, fields and hiking trails.

Privies and enclosed picnic shelters with stoves and firewood are maintained for winter use in the Chignecto ski area and Headquarters Camp-

PARKS CANADA

Snowshoers head out

ground. For the more adventurous, an overnight cabin is available on a free reservation basis at Laverty Hill. Fundy's deeply carved topography makes snowshoeing a necessary alternative to skiing in many places. Winter equipment is not available for sale or rent in the vicinity of the park. However, there is lodging. Bed-and-breakfast accommodations are open for winter business within a half-hour's drive.

Unserviced sites are available at no charge for winter campers in the Headquarters Campground. Nearby are heated washrooms with warm water. Group interpretive programs may be arranged for those who phone or write in advance.

Winter with its snow, ice, frosts and mists is a beautiful time of year to visit the park. Animals may not always be visible, but their tracks tell stories about what they are, where they have been, what they are eating and where they are sheltering.

IN PARTING

Two most important things to remember about your visits to Fundy: your use of the park must be nonconsumptive, and you must not interfere with other people's enjoyment of the park. Play an instrument, but play it softly. Take it easy, but take nothing else.

Should you require further information, clarification or updating, please speak to park personnel, or write to:

The Superintendent
Fundy National Park
P. O. Box 40,
Alma, New Brunswick
E0A 1B0
Or phone (506) 887-2000.

READING LIST

Allardyce, Gilbert. *The Salt and the Fir: Report on the History of the Fundy Park Area*. Ottawa: Parks Canada document, 1969.

Berrill, Michael, and Berrill, Deborah. *The North Atlantic Coast, Cape Cod to Newfoundland*. A Sierra Club Naturalist Guide. San Francisco: Sierra Club Books, 1981.

Burzynski, Michael P., and Marceau, Anne. *Fundy, Bay of the Giant Tides*. Alma, N.B.: A Fundy Guild publication, 1984.

Clark, Andrew Hill. *Acadia, the Geography of Early Nova Scotia to 1760*. Madison, Wisconsin: University of Wisconsin Press, 1968.

Dilworth, T., ed. *Land Mammals of New Brunswick*. Fredericton, N.B. T. Dilworth, 1984.

Forrester, Warren D. *Canadian Tide Manual*. Ottawa: Dept. of Fisheries and Oceans, 1983.

Gorham, Stanley W. *The Amphibians and Reptiles of New Brunswick*. Saint John, N.B.: New Brunswick Museum publication, 1970.

Gosner, Kenneth L. *A Field Guide to the Atlantic Seashore, from the Bay of Fundy to Cape Hatteras*. Boston, Mass.: Peterson Field Guide Series, Houghton Mifflin, 1979.

Leim, A. H., and Scott, W. B. *Fishes of the Atlantic Coast of Canada*. Ottawa: Fisheries Research Board of Canada, 1966.

Majka, Mary. *Fundy National Park*. Fredericton, N.B.: Brunswick Press, 1977.

"The Rocks," Hopewell Cape

Squires, W. Austin. *The Birds of New Brunswick*. Saint John, N.B.: New Brunswick Museum Publication, 1976.

Waterman, Laura, and Waterman, Guy. *Backwoods Ethics, Environmental Concerns for Hikers and Campers*. Washington, D.C.: Stone Wall Press, 1980.

Watts, May Theilgaard. *Reading the Landscape, an Adventure in Ecology*. Toronto: Collier-Macmillan Canada, 1968.

Wright, Bruce S. *The Eastern Panther, a Question of Survival*. Toronto: Clarke, Irwin, 1972.

Booklets, brochures and other information about Canada's National Parks, National Historic Parks and Heritage Canals can be obtained free of charge from Parks Canada, Information Services, 10 Wellington Street, Hull, Quebec K1A 1G2.

INDEX

aboiteaux, 118
Acadians, 75–77
accommodation, 93–94, 120–121
acid rain, 25
Albert county, 81, 85, 116–120; museum, 117
Albert Mines, village of, 117
Albert oil shales, 13, 117
Albert, village of, 118–119
Alma, Beach, 22, 24, 28, 30, 36, 37, 91; River. See rivers, Upper Salmon; village of 17, 79, 80, 81, 82, 85, 119–20
amphibians, 48, 69, 73, 97
Appalachian Mtns., 9, 32
Atlantic Ocean, 15, 28, 29, 30, 31
autumn, 24, 45

Bay of Fundy. See Fundy, Bay of
beaches, 32, 33, 119
bear, 56, 109, 112
beaver, 52, 53, 73, 97, 101, 116
beech bark canker, 44
Bennett Brook Trail, 68, 108
Bennett Lake, 72, 115
berries, 108, 109
bicycling, 113
Big Dam, 12, 65, 105
bioluminescence, 37, 45
birch dieback, 44
birdwatching, 114
birds, 49–50; migration of, 24, 97; of prey, 50; seabirds, 114, 115, 119; shorebirds, 119; songbirds, 40, 89, 115

blackflies, 69
Black Hole Trail, 107
boating, 115
bobcat, 53, 55, 97
bog, 72, 73, 97, 109
Boss Point Formation, 14, 15
brainworm, 50–51
British settlers, 78
budworm. See spruce budworm

Caledonia Highlands, 9
campgrounds, 93–94; primitive, 104
Cannon Town, 79, 80
Cape Enrage, 14, 119
Caribou Plain Trail, 72, 91, 97, 110, 115
caribou, woodland, 41, 72, 79
carnivorous plants, 73, 97, 105, 116
caves, 54, 100, 117
Chambers Lake, 107
Champlain, Samuel de, 75, 76
Chignecto Bay, 27, 30
clams. See shellfish
climate, 19–25
clubmosses, 45
Coastal Trail, 91, 104
Coppermine Trail, 97, 114
cougar. See panther
covered bridges, 65, 91, 116, 117
Cove Trail, 97
coyote, 53, 55, 57, 58

dams, 72, 82–83, 101, 105
DDT, 59

deer, 23, 41, 50–51, 101, 112, 116
Dennis Beach, 24, 119
Devil's Half Acre, 54, 91, 96
Dickson Falls Trail, 96

East Branch Trail, 100

ferns, 42, 45
fields, 88–89
fish, freshwater, 63, 68, 69–70, 82, 86; marine, 35, 37. *See also* salmon
fishing, 115
fishwatching, 113–114
flowers. *See* plants
fog, 20, 21
forest, 39–47; Acadian, 9, 39, 40, 45; hardwood, 42–45; mixed, 47; softwood, 40–42, 45, 61
Forks Trail, 106
fossils, 14
Foster Brook Trail, 104
Fortyfive Road, 80, 116
Fundy, Bay of, 13, 16, 19, 27, 28, 30–32
fungi, 42, 44, 45, 46

geology, 11–17
glaciation, 17, 31, 32
golf course, 17, 112
Goose River Trail, 107
Groundhog Day Gale, 21

handicapped, facilities for, 112
Hastings, Road, 115; Settlement, 81
Harvey, 118, 119
Headquarters Area, 17
Herring Cove, 13, 14, 67, 80, 81, 86, 100
hiking, 96–112
Hillsborough, 13, 117
Hopewell, Cape, 13, 117; Conglomerate, 13, 15

ice ages. *See* glaciation
ice storms, 22, 23, 45
Immigrant Road. *See* Shepody Road
Indians, 75, 76, 77
interpretation program, 92, 94–95
insects, 47–48, 53, 68. *See also* spruce budworm
intertidal life, 32–35, 37
invertebrates, 47

kame terrace, 17

kettle lake, 17, 72
Kinnie Brook Trail, 101

lakes, 72, 73
Laverty, Falls Trail, 105; Lake, 116; Road, 81, 116
lichens, 40
lobster. *See* shellfish
Louisbourg, Fortress of, 39, 76
loyalists, 78
lumber industry, 39, 79, 82–85

MacLaren Pond, 17, 72, 114
mammals, terrestrial, 41, 50–57, 58, 61; marine, 36
Maple Grove Road, 115
marine life, 35–37. *See also* intertidal life
Matthews Head, 53, 81, 91, 97
marshes. *See* salt marsh
marten, 58, 61
Martin Head, 15
Marven Lake Trail, 107
Marys Point, 119
Minas Basin, 27, 30
mining, 85
Moncton, 116
moose, 23, 41, 50–52, 73, 87, 109, 110, 116
Moosehorn Trail, 106
mosses, 42, 72
mushrooms. *See* fungi

national parks, 8–9, 61
New Brunswick, 78, 81

Owls Head, 14

paralytic shellfish poisoning, 37
panther, eastern, 56, 57, 58
Parks Canada, 8
peregrine falcon, 59–60, 92, 115
Petitcodiac River, 31, 116
pets, 116
plants, bog, 72–73; field, 88–89; forest, 40–47; orchids, 69, 89, 92; riverside, 68, 101, 104; spring flowers, 42, 69
Point Wolfe, 13, 59, 60, 91; mill, 79, 82, 84, 85; River, 58
poison ivy, 68, 109
porcupine, 41, 42, 54–56, 96, 116
Port Royal, 76
Potato Famine, 81

privateers, 76, 77
prospecting, 97

raccoon, 54, 96, 109
Rattail Trail, 108
recreation, 96–108, 112–16
Red Head, 119
red tide, 37
regulations, 53, 109, 112, 113
reptiles. *See* snakes
rivers, 12, 63–73, 92
Riverside-Albert. *See* Albert, village of
Rocks Provincial Park, The, 13, 32, 117

Saint John, 78, 79
Salem-Hillsborough Railway, 117
salmon, 58–59, 63, 69–70, 82, 92, 104, 115
Salmon River, village of, see Alma
salt marsh, 27–28, 107, 118–19
scallops. *See* shellfish
scenic drives, 115, 116
sea smoke, 22
seaweeds, 34, 35, 37
services, 120
Shaded Maples Trail, 97, 115
shellfish, 36–37, 120
Shepody, Bay, 78, 119; Road, 78, 80, 81, 116, 120; settlement, 76
shipbuilding, 84–86

shoreline erosion, 30–32
Sieur de Monts, 76
skiing, 120
snakes, 48–49, 88
soils, 25, 73, 81, 85, 88, 111
spruce budworm, 23, 40–41
Squaws Cap, 91, 104
Stoney Creek, 116–117
Sussex, 13
swimming, 24, 113

Third Vault Trail, 101
tidal bore, 116
tides, 27–34, 111
Tracey Lake Trail, 108
trails. *See* hiking
trees, 39–47
trout. *See* fish

Upper Salmon River Trail, 92, 105

water, drinking, 109
waterfalls, 65–67, 83, 92, 96, 100, 101, 105–106
Waterside, 15, 24, 119
weather. *See* climate
weirs, 36–37, 82
Whitetail Trail, 101
winter activities, 120–121
Wolfe Lake, 71

Canada